EDITION LIPP

Matthias Gretzschel
David Menzhausen

DRESDEN

a guide to the
Saxon State Capital

with an introductory essay by
Dr. Joachim Menzhausen
Director of the Green Vault

Karl M. Lipp Verlag München

Imprint:

8000 Munich 71, Meglingerstr. 60
Tel.: 089/785808-0, Fax: 089/78580833

Made and printed by:
Lipp GmbH, Graphische Betriebe, Munich

Graphic design and arrangement: Siegmar Schamm

ISBN 3-87490-917-4

Photographs by the courtesy of:

Colour photos: Werner Lieberknecht, Ulrich Kerth
Black-and-white photos: Markus Gretzschel
Saxon Landesbibliothek, Abt. Deutsche Fotothek: Pages 10-18
Drawings: Hans Mokroß

Dresden's Splendour

The traveller's first impression of Dresden is not one of splendour. The difference between the reputation of the town and its appearance is alarming. The Saxon Residence town was considered to be one of the most beautiful and cleanest places on the Continent. Art museums and opera, as well as the surrounding low mountain range had attracted visitors from the very beginnings of tourism, so the city was well provided with excellent hotels, restaurants, art dealers, concert halls and theatres. On February 13th 1945 the Royal Air Force carried out its heaviest air-raid of the Second World War – on the historic city centre. In spite of the experts' protests the Communist rulers pulled down the still majestic ruins of numerous buildings and streets, all part of German art history; they were replaced by a depressing vision of a Socialist industrial town. Even these buildings, as everything else, were neglected, and this is what the dismayed visitor sees first.

This town should not be looked at on a hurried sightseeing tour; visitors should enjoy the view of the Elbe valley from the Brühlsche Terrace,amazed that there is still a river in Europe that flows through a city between meadows, with waterfowl resting on the sandbanks. From here you can see the surrounding woods and vineyards, an important characteristic of this place. From the Brühlsche Terrace you enter the Albertinum,the old Electoral Saxon Arsenal, now late 19th century style; it houses, provisionally, the Dresden Gallery and the Green Vault (Grünes Gewölbe). On the middle floor is a permanent exhibition of the Saxon Treasure Chamber, in which about half of the stock is on show. The visitor cannot help sensing the splendour of this town. For even half of the Green Vault is unique, at least in magnificence, abundance and elegance incomparable with any other royal treasure chamber on the Continent. The original eight rooms of this collection, in which the objects were arranged according to materials, have now been reduced to four in the Albertinum, but you can see parts of the initial arrangements with which King August the Strong built up this first public treasure chamber museum in the world at the beginning of the 18th. century – in miniature, as it were, with sections for silver and gold, ivory, amber, semi-precious stones, preciosities, cabinet-pieces and crown jewels. Both the court goldsmith Dinglinger's great works of art and the royal sets of jewellery are unsurpassed in size and quality. It is not by chance that all these craftsmen lived during the reign of the two Saxon kings from Poland (1697-1763). August the Strong was the greatest patron of the arts in the history of German culture, and it was he above all who made Dresden into the "Florence on the Elbe", as Herder called it. His son August III, however, was one of the most important European collectors of paintings and he founded the world-wide reputation of the Dresden Opera and its orchestra, the Dresden State Orchestra of today. The Dresden Gallery of old and new masters has been packed into the upper floor of the Albertinum. This will remain so until 1992 when the reconstruction of Gottfried Semper's gallery building at the north end of the Zwinger will be finished. Masterpieces of European painting, mentioned in every history of art, hang here almost as in a depot. Italian renaissance and Dutch baroque paintings of such quality can hardly be seen in one place anywhere else on earth; for it is a feature of the Dresden Gallery that it is, among the great galleries on the Continent, perhaps small but perhaps the finest. The knowledge of the two royal collectors was just as outstanding as the means at their disposal. They included only the best works in their gallery.

The influence of these works of art in Dresden is shown by paintings of later artists. The greatest German Romantic landscape painter, Caspar David Friedrich, wrote that he came to Dresden because of the beautiful natural surroundings and the superb art collections. In the Paintings Gallery of New Masters several of his best pictures are on show, as also works by French and eminent German Impressionists (Liebermann, Slevogt, Corinth), paintings by the Brücke artists and by Otto Dix, who was a pupil and teacher at the Academy on the Brühlsche Terrace. The world-famous views of Dresden by the court painter Bernardo Bellotto, called Canaletto, hang in front of the main stairway up to the gallery. They show the town at the peak of its splendour – since 1945 lost to the world. The soaring dome of the Church of Our Lady (Frauenkirche), which crowns the town in Bellotto's paintings, still lies not far from the Albertinum, a monstrous heap of rubble among remains of walls marking about a third of the height of the dome. This was the only giant stone cupola of post-antiquity on our continent, rising up in the shape of a slim bell to a height of 95 metres – a brilliant achievement of the Protestant town architect George Bähr, supported and patronized by August the Strong, who as ruler of a Lutheran country converted to Catholicism in order to attain the Polish crown. Later, his son built the Catholic Court Church (Hofkirche) between the Castle and the Augustus Bridge on the bank of the Elbe; it is now the cathedral of the Dresden-Meissen diocese. No other town in Europe possessed such magnificent churches of the two main denominations during the Counter-Reformation era. The Saxon kings of Poland, at the same time Electors of Lutheran Saxony, made this amazing combination possible, which seems to be a precursor of the ecumenical movement to-day; it marks the beginning of the liberalism of the Enlightenment and that is Saxony's best heritage. A second huge ruined building, between the Catholic Court Church and the Zwinger, characterizes to-day's view of the town. It is the Residence Castle of Saxony's Electors and kings of the House of Wettin. But at present it is being rebuilt. The working model of the building is on show in the west wing and even a visitor with little knowledge must realize that this, together with the Hofburg in Vienna and the Residence in Munich, was the third great renaissance castle in central Europe – and will be again. Built in the middle of the 16th century as the first castle of the Holy Roman Empire to have four uniform wings, it represented the Protestant power in North Europe. After completion in a few years' time it will be easy to make out Dresden's splendour from the Castle Square (Schloßplatz), then closed in by Semper's rebuilt Opera, his Gallery and the adjoining Zwinger, the Castle, the Catholic Court Church and the high banks of the Elbe River.

The Zwinger, named after the space between two fortress walls, was originally August the Strong's orangery, then the arena for his festivals and

Panorama of Dresden

Ruins of the Church of Our Lady in front of Dome of the Art Society

finally the building for the scientific museums he had founded. His first architect Matthäus Daniel Pöppelmann built it between 1709 and 1719. It is the most fantastic and dynamic late baroque building in the whole of Europe, the result of the close cooperation between the architect and the great sculptor Balthasar Permoser. We today sense the structural affinity to the Green Vault: splendour and elegance, opulence and delicacy, northern austerity and southern exuberance – a unique combination. For the century-old enmity between the Catholic South and the Protestant North of the Continent was ended here and the two great cultural movements in Europe united.

The Japanese Palace lies in a little park on the Neustadt bank of the Elbe, diagonally opposite the Castle Square. August the Strong had it put up for his porcelain collection; this is now housed in the Zwinger. In spite of numerous earlier donations and considerable losses during the Second World War it is still the largest of its kind. No other museum can present Chinese and Japanese porcelain from the decades around 1700 and early Meissen porcelain in such quantity and quality. In 1708 Johann Friedrich Böttger had, in his laboratory on the Brühlsche Terrace, invented hard porcelain. The first products of the Saxon State Manufactory, founded in the Albrechtsburg in Meissen in 1710, were Böttger stoneware and Böttger porcelain, as well as the large white porcelain animals created after 1730 by the sculptors Kirchner and Kaendler; they now belong to the rarities in the great museums of the world. But of course the Dresden Collection possesses a large number of these works of art and exhibits them in one of its rooms in the Zwinger. It is the aim of the experts, however, one day to return the collection to the Japanese Palace that was built specially for it. This is by the river, as is the first European chinoisery-castle Pillnitz further up, and Moritzburg Castle on the plateau to the north of the town. That is typical of August the Strong's castles, they are in close connection with the surrounding countryside but without dominating it. This close connection between architecture and landscape suggested itself in a region as beautiful as this – between the Lausitz Hills, "Saxon Switzerland" and the Erzgebirge (Ore-Mountains) – with the slopes down into the wide river valley which continually opens up different angles of view. The visitor who stays here longer soon realizes that the town has its own typical light, as characteristic as the white light in New York or the silver-grey of Paris. Here it is blue-grey, produced by the mist over the river and the location between the hills. It makes the distance hazy in the mist and surrounds the towers of the town and the castles in the meadows with a soft veil, as depicted again and again by the great painters who lived here.

Dresden is the most maltreated town in Germany. But it is possible that in the near future even the short-time visitor will feel the charm of Dresden and keep the memory of its splendour – if the Germans are wise.

Dr. Joachim Menzhausen

The State Art Collections

As other collections in European capitals the Dresden State Art Collections resulted from the interest, engagement and love of art, over centuries, of the Saxon Electors and kings. Their ability as collectors and patrons is proved by the high quality of the works of art. Although the Dresden collections are not the largest, compared with other European museums, their quality is unsurpassed.
The history of the Art Collections begins really with the relics collection of Friedrich the Wise, Martin Luther's patron and protector. But the basis of the future Collections was the art chamber that August I founded in 1560. During the following centuries the collection increased steadily. However, it was August the Strong who started collecting works of art in Dresden on a large scale. In 1724 the Green Vault was opened to the public; this Saxon treasure chamber was the first in the world to be arranged according to artistic methods.
During the 18th, 19th and beginning of the 20th centuries the continually increasing stock, with its origins in the art chamber, was divided up into several individual museums supervised by experts. We will never get over the inconceivable bombing of Dresden in the Second World War. On February 13th 1945 bombs destroyed almost all the historic buildings in the town centre. Luckily the losses were not too heavy in the collections, which had been evacuated. Afterwards the art treasures were taken to Russia "for security reasons" and returned in 1958.
Because the Communist government wanted to turn Dresden into a "new Socialist city" most of the rebuilding must be considered to be unsuccessful and destructive. It was only thanks to the curators' and art historians' intensive urging and efforts that a part of Dresden's splendour returned, not only in the collections but in the city too. The collections cannot be fully displayed until the rebuilding of the Dresden Castle has been completed at the end of the millennium.

Green Vault***

Albertinum, Georg-Treu-Platz
8012 Dresden Tel. 495 30 56
Closed on Thursdays

The treasure chamber of the Saxon Electors and kings is doubtless the one Dresden museum that fascinates even the visitor with little knowledge of art history. It shows a unique symbiosis of art and an exceptional craftsmanship, in conjunction with the most beautiful, precious and valuable materials in the world. When Dresden's splendour is spoken of, it is here in the Green Vault that it can best be seen. The name Green Vault is derived from the once green vault of the "secret safekeeping" in the Dresden Castle. It originated in the art chamber that Elector August had founded in 1560 – a kind of universal museum. It showed the most interesting results of science and technology, as well as masterpieces of craftsman-

Giovanni Bologna: Mercury

ship. Paintings and sculptures played only a minor role. This stock increased over the years until August the Strong converted it, partially from 1723-1729, into the first treasure chamber in the world to be open to the general public. As the original rooms in the Castle are still being restored, the Green Vault has, since 1959, been housed in the Albertinum – showing about half of its stock in four rooms there.

Room 1: On show here are elaborate objects made of silver and German semi-precious stones, and several bronzes. The optical attraction on the right side is the reconstructed silver wall; its superabundance of baroque treasures gives an impression of the original treasure chamber atmosphere. Other main works are the writing cascet by the famous Nuremberg master Wenzel Jamnitzer, as well as bronzes by Giovanni Bologna and Adrian de Vries.

Room 2: Here the visitor can see ivory, amber and works of art in semi-precious stones both of Italian origin and tradition. Some of the most important objects are the elaborate ones of ivory and of fascinating rock crystal and the over 2-metre-high cabinet made of amber. It was made in Königsberg and came to Dresden in 1728 as a present from the Prussian king.

Room 3: The exhibits in this room are primarily works by the jeweller Johann Melchior Dinglinger and the sculptor Balthasar Permoser from the first third of the 18th century. The central position is taken up by the "Imperial Household of the Great Mogul", the most brilliant European jeweller's work of art of the baroque period. 165 objects of solid, enamelled gold, studded with over 5000 diamonds and other jewels, describe the birthday of the Indian ruler Aureng Zeb on a stage-like kind of a palace-construction.

Room 4: Almost the complete Saxon crown jewels are on display here. The 9 sets of jewellery of the Saxon-Polish kings are a surprise. Worth mentioning is also the famous green diamond (41-carat) and one of the biggest sapphires (648-carat) ever to be found.

Paintings Gallery Old Masters***

until 1992 in the Albertinum
Brühlsche Terrasse
8012 Dresden,
Tel. 495 23 81
Closed on Mondays

J. M. Dinglinger: August the Strong's gold coffee set

The Imperial Household in Delhi on the Great Mogul's Birthday (detail).

The Dresden Paintings Gallery also originated from the treasure chamber that was founded in 1560. After the end of the Nordic War, August the Strong had 535 paintings brought into the Castle, the most famous of them being Giorgione's "Slumbering Venus". The actual founding of the Gallery took place in 1722 when he had an inventory made of all the paintings and put them together in the stable building at the Jüdenhof (see Johanneum).

Whereas August the Strong was mainly interested in architecture, valuables and porcelain, it is to his son August III that Dresden owes the world-famous collection of pictures.
To an even greater extent than his father he sent agents all over Europe to buy well-known pictures and entire collections. Liotard's "Chocolate Girl" came to Dresden in 1741, as well as 268 pictures from the Wallenstein Collection on Dux Castle which included Vermeer van Delft's "Matchmaker" and two small paintings by Franz Hals. In 1742 there followed 84 paintings from the imperial gallery in Prague, Rubens' "Wild Boar Hunt" and Tintoretto's "Women Playing Music". After long negotiations, one of the most important purchases was that of the Duke of Modena's collection – it included Tizian's "Interest Groschen", Holbein's "Portrait of Morette", Andrea del Sarto's "Abraham's Sacrifice", Carraci's "Lute Player", three pictures by Velazquez and four panels by Corregio. The works were mostly bought in Paris and Antwerp and at the trade fair in Leipzig.

One of the last, but at the same time most significant and expensive, purchases of the gallery at this period, was that of Raffael's "Sistine Madonna", for which extensive negotiations were necessary. Over the following centuries this painting symbolized the world fame of the Dresden Gallery. The Seven Years' War (1756-63) put an end to the gallery's decisive phase of development. Of course the 19th century saw further purchases but they did not change the character of the collection to any extent.

Albrecht Dürer: The Dresden Altar

In the middle of the 19th century it was impossible to further enlarge the stable building at the Jüdenhof. Gottfried Semper was commissioned with the construction of the Gallery at one end of the still unfinished Zwinger, facing the Elbe.

After completion of the reconstruction work in 1992 the Collection will again be on show in this building.

Paintings Gallery New Masters**

Albertinum, Brühlsche Terrasse
8012 Dresden, Tel. 4953056
At present closed on Mondays

Until the end of the 19th century only little, and if then regional, contemporary art was purchased for the Gallery. Then under the directorship of the art historian Karl Woermann a start was made "to illustrate the development of art history in the

Tizian: The Interest Groschen

Raffael: The Sistine Madonna

19th century with its various trends and particularly to do justice to the progressing present". Paintings by Adolph Menzel, Fritz von Uhde, Hans Thoma, Arnold Böcklin, Carl Spitzweg and the Dresdener Gotthardt Kuehl were among the first to be bought by Woermann. The Dresden gallery acquired its first French Impressionist work in 1909, Monet's "Seine bank near Lavacourt". Although he had only modest funds at his disposal and few donations, the ambitious gallery director slowly put his plans into effect. But in these first years it had already been clear which would be the future special fields: German Romanticism, Impressionism and the Realism of the second half of the 19th century.

When the only 30-year-old Hans Posse took over the Gallery in 1910, its financial situation began to improve considerably, due to the founding of two new art associations. The collection was substantially enlarged with Romantic artists such as Carl Blechen, Clausen Dahl and the famous Caspar David Friedrich, as well as German Impressionists (Corinth, Liebermann and Slevogt). Later, works from beyond the German borders were acquired: E. Manet, C. Monet, E. Degas, A. Renoir, H. Toulouse-Lautrec, P. Gaugin and others. At the same time the Expressionists and representatives of Classical Modern art were gradually

C. D. Friedrich: The Cross in the Mountains

added to the Gallery. Thus when the "Gallery New Masters" was opened up as a separate museum in 1931 an excellent collection had been put together – unfortunately only for a short while. The National Socialist campaign "Degenerate Art" left a void in the 20th century stock, and on top of that there were several war losses. After 1945 the wrong communist purchasing policy and the lack of foreign currency meant that only a few of the gaps could be closed. However, in addition to superb 19th century pictures there are again important Expressionists, in particular the famous "War Triptych" by Otto Dix. Included is of course art

Otto Dix: War

from the former DDR, especially some good works of the Dresden School.

Porcelain Collection***

Zwinger
8012 Dresden Tel. 4952381
Closed on Fridays

The coincidence of two facts led to the founding of the world-famous Porcelain Collection in Dresden. The Elector of Saxony and King of Poland said of himself that he pined for porcelain – and in Dresden Johann Friedrich Böttger invented European hard porcelain in 1708. Böttger came to the Saxon court as an alchemist in 1701, and remained until shortly before his early death a prisoner of the king – in order to keep the secret of porcelain manufacturing.

The discovery of porcelain was not pure chance, for in 1704 Böttger, together with the scientist Ehrenfried Walther von Tschirnhaus, carried out specific experiments with ceramic materials. In 1710 the king founded the first European porcelain manufactory in Meissen, a town 25 km from Dresden. Since that time the most beautiful and exquisite pieces from the manufactory came to the royal collection.

Böttger stoneware vase with lid, 1716

The history of the Porcelain Collection began in 1717 when August the

J. G. Kirchner: Lioness

Strong bought a palace on the Neustadt side of the Elbe, which he planned to turn into a palace for porcelain (see Japanese Palace). Unfortunately he was not able to carry out this fantastic idea, for he died in 1733 – only the plans in the Saxon Main State Archives and 20 000 porcelain objects in the Zwinger are a reminder of it. As fashion and taste were subject to change, the Collection led a shadowy existence until 1876 when it was moved to new rooms on the upper floor of the old Gallery building (Johanneum). Since 1962 it has been on show, flooded with light in the halls and galleries of the Zwinger. Chinese and Japanese porcelain items from the time around 1700 are on display, including the famous "Dragoon Vases", the largest collection at all of Böttger stoneware and Böttger porcelain, unique pieces with painting by Höroldt and more than 100 almost lifesize figures of animals by the sculptors Kirchner and Kändler.

Figurine of August the Strong

Historical Museum***

Zwinger, Semperbau
8012 Dresden, Tel. 495 23 81
Closed until 1992 due to reconstruction

This name is somewhat misleading for it is not a museum of history, but one of the most important collections in the world of arms and armoury of the highest artistic value and craftsmanship. As with other ruling houses, the House of Wettin, over the centuries, kept valuable weapons, armour etc. Under Elector Moritz (1541-53) an administrator was appointed for the first time. His successor, Elector August (1553-86), began to systematically increase the stock.

An excellent collection of this kind was part of the image of the electorial houses and the one in Dresden could certainly keep up with the imperial collection in Vienna. A handwritten inventory from the year 1606 contains 1500 pages. Up until the beginning of August the Strong's regency (1691) the collection continued to grow with major items, only to enter into a phase of relative passivity, for in the 18th century, the Age of Enlightenment, art and science were favoured. Today the museum is in possession of about 10 000 articles, of which up till now approx. 5% have been exhibited in a room in the Semper Gallery. With 3000 rifles and pistols of almost all of

Silvergilded sheath

Crown Gate of the Zwinger

Pillnitz Castle, Hill Palace

the renowned gunsmiths from the 16th to 18th centuries and about 2200 swords, rapiers and daggers – especially of the 16th and 17th centuries – the Historical Museum is the best in the world. The collection of magnificent clothes, riding equipment and armour is also of the greatest significance – it can certainly be compared with Madrid, Moscow, Stockholm and Vienna. When the Dresden Castle has been rebuilt sometime about the turn of the millennium, the exhibition will be very much larger.

Print-room**

Güntzstr. 34
8019 Dresden Tel. 4593813
Visitors hall open Mon., Tues. and Wed.

When the print-room was founded in 1720 under August the Strong as a separate collection it already owned numerous prints by Jost Amman, Sebald Beham, Albrecht Dürer, Lucas van Leyden and many others. In 1727 it was moved to the Zwinger, and by the beginning of the Seven Years' War had, due to extensive purchases, increased its stock to about 130 000 sheets; it was exceeded at that time only by the Bibliothèque Nationale in Paris. As from 1856 it was housed in Gottfried Semper's new building at the Zwinger. With the help of Karl Woermann, who was at the same time director of the Paintings Gallery, it came into its second prime. The old gaps were closed with prints by Grünewald, Dürer, Cranach, Tiepolo, Piranesi, Goya and many others. At the same time the aim was to collect contemporary art. Woermann opened the collection to a large number of visitors. For this collection,too, the Nazi period and the war meant a break. The National Socialist government confiscated almost all the works of modern German art. Since 1959 the Etchings Collection has been housed in the former school of arts and crafts in the Güntzstrasse. In spite of the lack of foreign currency and the hostile attitude to modern art in the communist cultural bureaucracy, a very wise purchase policy led to the closing of these

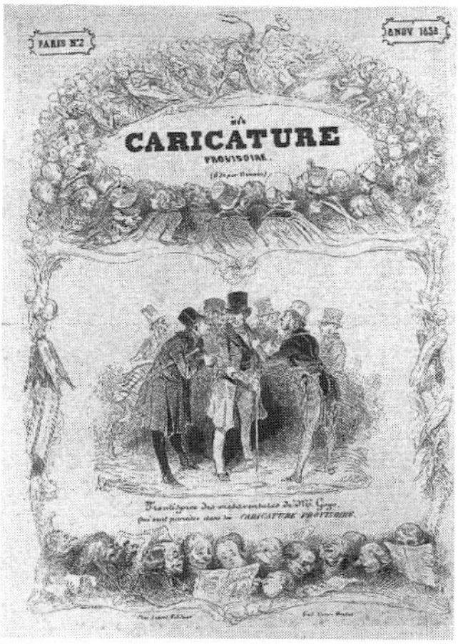

H. Daumier: Title page of "La Caricature"

gaps up to a certain degree. The high standard of this collection was not only kept up, in fact it was raised – even in the field of contemporary art. In addition to the visitors hall which is open to the public permanently, interesting parts of the collection are shown in alternating special exhibitions.

Museum of Decorative Arts Pillnitz Castle***

8057 Dresden Tel. 39325
Water Palace (Wasserpalais) closed on Mondays
Hill Palace (Bergpalais) closed on Tuesdays
The museum is open only from May until October

The Museum was founded in 1876 as a museum for arts and crafts. It was a department of the school of arts and crafts which had been opened a short time before and was supposed to impart knowledge to the students. The aim was to set aesthetic and technological criteria for skilled trade and the then up-and-coming industry which would lead to a new and better relationship between the producers and the consumers. For that reason entrance was free at the week-ends. The rapidly increasing stock was arranged according to fea-

Raeren stoneware, about 1600

tures of style and kinds of material. Unfortunately about half of the stock was lost in the Second World War. By means of the so-called castle retrieval campaign during the post-war years many important items were added to the museum. It was from this stock, together with numerous other objects, that the baroque castle Moritzburg was later

M. Koller: Large egg-shaped jar

furnished. Since 1963 the Museum has been located in Pillnitz Castle, where there are permanent exhibitions to be seen in the Water and Hill Palaces. Apart from the excellent handicrafts of glass, ceramics, silver, pewter and other materials, the furniture collection is also of great interest. It covers pieces from the 15th century until the present day, including, for example, works by Boulle, Risenburgh, Röntgen, East Asian furniture, Augsburg silver furniture and much else. For connoisseurs the collection of textiles – hardly known and unfortunately with little of its stock on show – is a particular attraction.

Sculpture Collection**

Albertinum, Georg-Treu-Platz
8012 Dresden Tel. 4953056
Closed on Thursdays

During the years 1723-26 August the Strong bought from the Prussian king Friedrich Wilhelm I the so-called "Brandenburg Collection", which mainly consisted of Roman busts. A little later there followed Duke Agostini Chigi's and Cardinal Albani's collections, including the Athena Lemnia, the so-named Dresden Zeus and Polyklet's Victorious Youth. The three "Herkulanerinnen", (full length statues of Roman ladies excavated in Herculaneum) were part of the estate of Prince Eugen of Savoy. For about a hundred years Dresden possessed Germany's leading collection of antiquities, which also inspired Johann Joachim Winckelmann to write his work on classicism. With Georg Treu, the distinguished expert on art, there began an important era for this collection. He bought smaller antiquities as well as 18th and 19th century sculptures, his friendship with Rodin and Meunier helping him to acquire particularly beautiful pieces for the Dresden collection. Since 1894 this collection has been in the Albertinum, the former arsenal, which was rebuilt especially for this purpose. Except through the campaign "Degenerate Art" (Lehmbruck, Barlach and Marcks) this museum hardly suffered war losses. However, it will not be until the Dresden Castle

The "Kleine Herculanerin"

has been rebuilt and the other museums have then moved out of the Albertinum that its many-sidedness and significance can again be fully appreciated. Some of the modern sculptures are being shown within the Gallery of New Masters. There is a permanent exhibition of old Saxon sculpture in the Albrechtburg in Meissen. The Sculpture Collection today in the Albertinum consists of works from the 3rd century BC up to the present.

Collection of Coins and Medals*

Albertinum, Georg-Treu-Platz
8012 Dresden Tel. 4953056
Closed on Thursdays

The collecting of coins dates back to the renaissance in Italy, where they were considered to be evidence of one's own great past. A little later it was the Humanists north of the Alps who were incited to collect coins by Italy and their preoccupation with antiquity. Merchants and princes who were interested in art emulated them. Thus in 1560 about 950 collections already existed in Europe. The one in Dresden is one of the oldest, for Duke Georg acquired the first coins during the first half of the 16th century. In the 18th century the collection flourished particularly well: in addition to being an intellectual entertainment, it was an essential source of the history of the royal houses.

The collection contains approx. 200 000 coins, medals and bank notes at present, the emphasis being on medieval and Saxon coins. For experts and specialized collectors there is, in addition to the exhibition, a room for studying purposes, a library and a hallmark stamp archive in the rooms of the former school of arts and crafts, Güntzstr. 34, which also houses the Collection of Engravings and the Central Art Library.

Folk Art Museum*

Jägerhof Castle, Köpckestr. 1
8060 Dresden Tel. 570817
Closed on Mondays

The museum is situated in Jägerhof Castle on the Neustadt side of the Elbe. At the end of th 19th century there were plans to found a collection in Dresden taking the Nordic Museum in Stockholm as a model. The first step was the founding of the "Society of Saxon Folklore" in 1897. After that it was mainly thanks to the longstanding engagement of the painter and professor at the Dresden Academy of Arts and Crafts, Oskar Seyffert, that the society with its already large stock became a museum in 1913.

The Dresden Folk Art Museum is one of the earliest foundings of this kind in Germany and specializes in Upper Saxon and Lausitz folk art. The numerous pieces of painted peasant furniture and the coloured ceramics, so typical of the individual regions, in the permanent exhibition are particularly impressive. The lovely collection of old toys on the upper floor is not only a delight for children. Each year in Advent there is a special exhibition of nutcrackers and other items typical of the Erzgebirge (Ore-Mountains), such as pyramids of hand-carved figures which move round continuously in circles when a candle underneath is lit.

Marionette Theatre Collection*

Barkengasse 6
8122 Radebeul Tel. 74373
Closed on Mon., Fri. and Sat.

This interesting special museum in the Hohenhaus in Radebeul originated from a private collection. The famous puppet show historiographer Otto Link got to know the eminent collector and medical doctor Prof. Dr. Arthur Kollmann after the First World War. This collection is the result of their joint work. It comprises today several ten thousands of items and gives a survey of puppet and figure shows of different peoples. The collection of puppets and sets of Saxon marionette theatres is of course particularly well represented and of great interest. Part of it can be seen in the permanent exhibition.

The Scientific and Technical Museums

The Mathematics-Physics Collection***

Zwinger
8012 Dresden, Tel. 4951364
Closed on Thursdays

This fascinating scientific museum originated, like most of the other collections, from the art chamber that Elector August founded in 1560. Thus the art chamber possessed 7500 tools and almost 500 scientific instruments as early as 1587. In 1728

Globe Clock, 1586

Planetary Orbit Clock, 1563-86

the "Royal Collection of Mathematical and Physical Instruments" was separated from the art chamber and housed in the still unfinished Zwinger. So the Mathematics-Physics Collection is the only Dresden museum that has remained in the same building and same rooms since the 18th century. Directly next to the ticket office there is the magnificent collection of terrestrial and celestial globes; with its 70 exhibits from 7 centuries it is one of the most exclusive of its kind. There follow geodesic instruments, instruments to determine lengths and measurements, meteorology, optics, astronomy and mathematics. All these instruments are fascinating not only due to their technical refinement but especially to their materials, to the beauty and at the same time effectiveness of their form. On the first floor is another highly interesting collection – of artistically decorated and automatic clocks.

Military Historical Museum*

Dr.-Kurt-Fischer-Platz 3
8060 Dresden, Tel. 5920
Closed on Mondays

Since 1972 the Military Historical Museum (until 1989 the DDR Army Museum) has been housed in the former 19th century Saxon arsenal, which was the home of the Saxon Army Museum before the Second World War. More than 7000 exhibits in spacious rooms and on grounds in the open air document military history from about 1400 until today. Included are, for example, the legendary first German submarine, built by Wilhelm Bauer in 1850, and very impressive Soviet fighter planes and helicopters of the most recent past.
One department of the museum is in Königstein Castle in the Elbsandstein Hills; it includes among other things the famous medieval cannon, the "Lazy Maid".

Transport Museum*

Johanneum, Augustusstr. 1
8012 Dresden Tel. 4953002
Closed on Mondays

This technical museum is one of the newer ones, founded in 1952. As successor to notable art museums, it is located in the Johanneum; this permanent exhibition covers all spheres of transport – with numerous original objects, sections, models and documentations; for example, it includes the "Muldenthal" locomotive with tender (1861) – it was in use for over 90 years. One of the former ways of travelling is illustrated by the special coach (1885) of the Saxon Royal Train: it is occupied by lifesize dummies in original costumes. You can also see early motorcars by Daimler and Benz, Panhard-Levassor, original old motorcycles, model ships, flying machines and trams.

German Hygiene Museum**

Lingnerplatz 1
8012 Dresden Tel. 4955080
Closed on Fridays

This largest hygiene museum in the world was founded after the 1st International Hygiene Exhibition in 1911 at the suggestion of and with the financial support of the pharmaceutical industrialist Karl August Lingner and opened in 1930. The architect Wilhelm Kreis designed the building, which was obviously influenced by the Bauhaus group of artists (1928-30).

The museum became world-famous for its "Glass Woman". In 15 rooms you can see models of human anatomy, suggestions for the prevention of and fight against Illness, sexual biology and sexual hygiene and of course AIDS prophylaxis.
The workshops here are still used to make visual aids, which are in great demand all over the world.
There are also two concert halls in this building, the Steinsaal and the Kongreßsaal, on account of their acoustics particularly suitable for concerts, as well as a medicinal plant garden and a herb garden on the south side of the museum.

Museum of Ethnology*

Japanese Palace, Karl-Marx-Platz
8060 Dresden Tel. 52591
Closed on Fridays

This museum has been in existence since the second half of the 19th century and is one of Europe's important ethnological collections. It owns about 75 000 items from all over the world, assembled by eminent explorers. Regular special shows supplement the permanent exhibition.

Prehistorical Museum

Japanese Palace, Karl-Marx-Platz
8060 Dresden, Tel. 52591
Closed on Fridays and Saturdays

This museum was opened in 1874 and was housed originally in the Castle and the Zwinger. In 1956 it was moved to the Japanese Palace. It consists of an interesting collection of prehistoric and early historic finds. The museum is at the same time research centre for ground preservation within Saxony.

Museum for the History of Dresden

Ernst-Thälmann-Str. 2
8010 Dresden, Tel. 4952302
Closed on Fridays

Since 1965 the museum for the history of the town has been set up in the house of the Saxon "Landstände" (a body of representatives of various classes in medieval provincial politics) which had been built in 1776. It owns interesting works of art and other material which documents the history of the town. A special exhibition is dedicated to the fire brigade. This exhibition revealed a communist conception of history and it is to be changed under the new director, who has been in office since 1990.

Museum of Zoology*

Zwinger, entrance Kronentor
8012 Dresden, Tel. 4952503
Closed on Thursdays and Fridays

The State Museum of Zoology originated from the Chamber of Art and Natural History (founded in 1560) and became an independent natural history museum in 1720. For a long time it was combined with the Museum of Ethnology, but since 1945 it has been an independent museum and research centre. The 5.5 million objects range from insects to mammels. The permanent exhibition "The Animal in the History of Civilization" illustrates the relationship between human beings and animals since primeval times; it also includes the most interesting specimens of this voluminous collection.

State Museum of Mineralogy and Geology*

Schloßplatz
8010 Dresden, Tel. 4952446
Closed on Mondays and Tuesdays

This museum also originated from the old Chamber of Art and Natural History. It has a stock of about 50 000 minerals and 350 000 fossils, as well as a library with approx. 30 000 books, maps and schematic descriptions. The emphasis is on Cretaceous and Tertiary formations in Central Europe and minerals from Saxony. Interesting fossils from all over the world and superb minerals are on show permanently.

Technical Museum

Reinhold-Becker-Str. 5
8053 Dresden, Tel. 35485
Closed on Sundays

The Technical Museum opened up in 1966. An impression is conveyed of scientific apparatus, precision engineering, photography and electronics. Apart from this, there is here an impressive special collection of 200 typewriters, the oldest from 1864. The rare, secret and 35 mm cameras are also worth mentioning, as well as the electronics and television technology of the DDR era.

Book Museum of the Saxon State Library

Marienallee 12
8060 Dresden, Tel. 52677
Closed on Sundays

The Book Museum offers more than 400 treasures for book-lovers. The most comprehensive Maya manuscript in the world, the "Codex Boernerianus" of the 9th century, the book of flowers by Maria Sibylla Merian and Dürer's sketch book are particularly famous.

Castles, Palaces and Public Buildings

Zwinger***

The Dresden Zwinger is the most important late baroque building in Germany. The unique cooperation between the eminent architect Matthäus Daniel Pöppelmann, the Bavarian sculptor Balthasar Permoser and the art-loving ruler August the Strong brought forth a building (planned as orangery and festival ground) that was to become the main architectural work of the baroque period in Saxony. The first plans,which the king himself drew and on which the architects based their planning, date back to the year 1709. In 1710 Pöppelmann went on journeys to Bohemia, Austria and Italy in order to collect information on the newest trends in European architecture. Building started that same year. The name "Zwinger" is a term used in fortresses and defines the space between the outer and inner ramparts, where the Zwinger is in fact situated. The Zwinger Lake was made out of the former moat.

It was the first time that the fortifications at this spot were reduced, against the protests of the military; half a century later, during the Seven Years' War, this proved to be a fatal mistake.

In 1718 the Wall Pavilion, the Mathematics-Physics Collection building, the French Pavilion, the Kronentor (Crown Gate) and their galleries were almost finished. However, these buildings were supposed to play a central part in the celebrations on the occasion of the marriage between the Electoral prince and the Habsburg emperor's daughter Maria Josepha. That is why the Glockenspielpavillon (Carillon Pavilion) facing the town and the side with the royal lodge facing the Elbe were built in haste-made, provisionally, of wood. Whereas the parts of the Zwinger facing the town were erected in stone over the following years, the part facing the Elbe was left as it was. Pöppelmann had plans for a park and fountains from the Zwinger down to the Elbe.

In 1728 it was decided not to use the Zwinger as an orangery, and the king ordered the collections which had been separated from the Art Chamber to be transferred to the Zwinger, thus creating a "palace of the sciences".

It is impossible now to say exactly when Permoser took on the overall resonsibility for the sculptural embellishment of the building. But it is certain that the Crown Gate was the

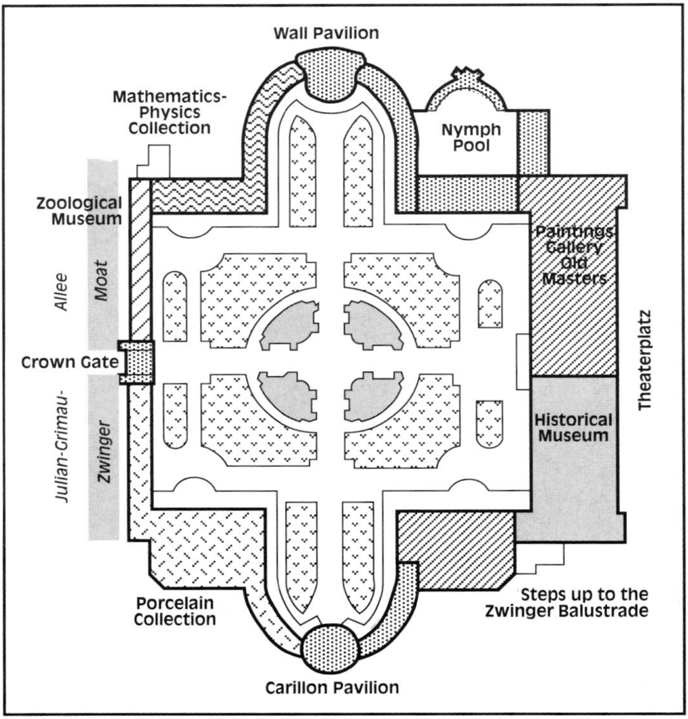

View of a cascade on the Long Gallery

result of the close cooperation between sculptor and architect. Here at the Zwinger architecture and sculpture are united in such a fantastic way as is hardly to be seen anywhere else.

Interest was lost in this outstanding edifice over the following generations, due to the changing prevailing tastes. It was not until the middle of the 19th century that the Zwinger was completed – with Gottfried Semper's Gallery Building (1847-55) in the style of the Italian renaissance. Almost completely destroyed in 1945, the Zwinger (as the first historic monument in Dresden) was rebuilt by 1963.

Residence Castle and Taschenberg Palace**

A castle complex in Dresden was first mentioned as "castrum" about 700

Zwinger

Residence Castle, Stable Court

years ago. A closed-in four-wing castle was built at the end of the 15th century. After Saxony had been divided up between the brothers Ernst and Albrecht in 1485, the so-called "Leipzig Division", Dresden became the princely capital of the Albertiner; the title of Elector remained with the Ernestiner (today Saxony-Anhalt, Thuringia) until the middle of the 16th century, when Duke Moritz with his tactical policy managed to attain it. The castle complex was considerably enlarged (1548-56). This part of the building, with excellent renaissance architecture, can best be seen today in the large castle court with its sandstone reliefs of the highest quality. At the end of the 16th century there followed the "Stallhof" (Stable Court) with its 100 m long colonnade, the Toscan architecture of which is decorated with the coats of arms of the Saxon regions. It was probably designed by Giovanni Maria Nosseni, who also created the bronze pillars on the Ringelstechbahn (ring-shooting course). On the outside of the long passage (Augustusstr.) there is the 102 m long Fürstenzug (Parade of Princes); all the dukes of the House of Wettin are portrayed in a long procession of mounted rulers, followed by representatives of science and art (93 people in all). The Saxon painter Wilhelm Walther, who depicted himself as the last person in the row, had originally used the sgraffito technique (1872-76). As early as 1900, however, considerable damage became apparant, so the 957 sq m mural was transferred by the Meissen Porcelain Manufactory onto 25000 porcelain tiles, and put up again in 1907. Considerable parts of the castle had been destroyed by fire in 1701, and not rebuilt until 1717-19 during the reign of August the Strong. The 2nd floor rooms were redecorated in baroque style during his reign, as was the Green Vault (1723-29); this was the first museum in Europe considered to be a complete work of art as such.
On the occasion of the 800th anniversary celebrations of the House of Wettin the castle was renovated to a large extent (1889-1901) – this time in neo-renaissance style. During the

Partial view Turkish Fountain in front of Castle

bombing in 1945 the castle was gutted. Apart from securing measures during the 1960's, the building remained a ruin until 1986. In that year extensive reconstruction work was started, which should be finished at the turn of the millennium. Then the castle will be used by the State Art Collections as a museum building. In addition to the alternating exhibitions in the old rooms of the Green Vault, only the Stable Court is open to the public at present. Adjoining the castle to the south are the ruins of the Taschenberg Palace, which was built from 1705-08 for August the Strong's mistress, Duchess Cosel. Alterations for the Electoral prince and his wife were made in 1718/19.
At present it is being considered whether it might later be turned into a luxury hotel.

Semper Opera***

see Theatres p. 35

Guard-House in the Old Town

This building was erected in 1830-32 by Joseph Thürmer to the designs of

Karl Friedrich Schinkel. It is this famous architect's only building in Dresden, one of his late works. With a triangular gable on top of six ionic columns, it follows the form of Greek temples. The sculptures in the tympanum of this classical building are the work of Joseph Herrmann and Franz Pettrich. At present it houses the central theatre box office.

Japanese Palace**

It was built in 1715 by order of Count Flemming and was named after its first resident – Dutch Palace. It was probably in connection with the preparations for the celebrations of the marriage between the Electoral prince and the Habsburg emperor's daughter Maria Josepha that August the Strong bought this castle in 1717. These grand celebrations, some of which took place in this castle, are depicted on numerous engravings. It is possible that, during the celebrations, August the Strong thought of converting the palace into a porcelain castle, a grand work of art,entirely of porcelain. But later, 1727-33, it was turned into a prestigious four-wing building – a collective achievement of Jean de Bodt, Johann Christoph Knöffel, Zacharias Longuelune and Matthäus Daniel Pöppelmann. In 1732 work was started on the conversion into a porcelain castle. There were plans for arrangements of figures on the walls, plates and vessels, a throne and carillon made of Meissen porcelain, as well as a chapel with lifesize figures of saints.

The death of August the Strong (1733) put an end to the plans of completing this fantastic project – his son had other interests.
Today, only Benjamin Thomae's gable relief recalls August the Strong's dream – with the allegorical portrayal of the homage of the porcelain-manufacturing regions to the figure of Saxonia.
Together with the Electoral library it later took in the collection of antiquities and coins.
In 1836 Gottfried Semper designed the painting of several rooms in imitation of the classical style; these rooms on the ground floor were recently restored.
The Prehistorical Museum and the Museum of Ethnology are located in those rooms which have been restored after their destruction during the war.

Palace in the Large Garden**

The so-called Large Garden is 2 sq km in size, the largest park in Dresden. It was originally laid out during the second half of the 17th century under Elector Johann Georg II; later it became a typical example of 18th century Saxon landscape gardening, uniting the conceptions of the French ornamental garden and that of the English landscape garden. In 1873 it was given its final lay-out as an English landscape garden by

Japanese Palace

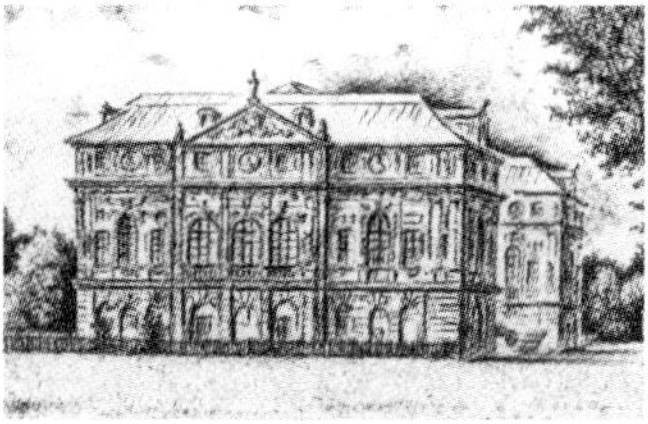
Palace in the Large Garden

Friedrich Bouché. At the intersection of the main avenues there is a palace, which ranks as one of the best German pieces of baroque architecture from the second half of the 17th century. It was built in 1678-83 to plans by Johann Georg Starcke, its H-shaped ground plan being a clear indication of the influence of French castles. The abundant sculptural decoration was the work of Abraham Conrad Buchau, Markus Conrad Dietze, Georg and Paul Heermann, as well as Jeremias and Konrad Max Süssner. Until 1945 the palace was a museum of (Saxon) antiquity; destroyed during the war, it has only been patched up on the outside. A complete renovation is planned.
Four of the original eight gentlemen's houses (J.G.Starcke, 1690) were rebuilt after the war.
The 3.50 m high sandstone group at the west end of the main avenue is by Balthasar Permoser (Hercules conquering King Busiris); the group of marble figures west of the palace is by Pietro Balestra (Time abducts Beauty). (Compare Park Railway p. 39)

Johanneum**

In 1586-91 Elector Christian I had a stable building,designed by Hans Irmisch and Paul Buchner in renaissance style, erected at the Neumarkt; its upper storey was used as a chamber for armaments and armour. In the 18th century the building was changed into baroque in two stages (1722-31 Georg Maximilian von Fürstenhoff, 1744-46 Johann Christoph Knöffel); it served from 1722 onwards as a picture gallery. After the paintings had been moved to the Semper gallery building in 1855, the Johanneum was used as an outbuilding for the royal carriages, the Historical Museum and the Porcelain Collection. After its destruction in the war and its rebuilding it has housed, since 1952, the Transport Museum. To the west of the Johanneum you can see the so-called "Beautiful Gate", built in about 1555 by Juan Maria da Padua and Hans Walther II as portal of the castle chapel. It is considered to be one of the most magnificent creations of the German renaissance.

Country House

This was Dresden's first large administration building, erected in 1770-76 by Friedrich August Krubsacius for the Saxon political bodies. The double flights of stairs, curving upwards inside the building,are particularly worth seeing. It was rebuilt by 1965, since when it has housed the Museum for the History of the Town.

New Town Hall

The architects Karl Roth and Edmund Bräter built the New Town Hall in 1904-10 for the Dresden town administration. The numerous offices of the town, which had grown rapidly at the end of the 19th century, had at last enough room in this spacious building complex. Of the delightful interior decoration, the stairway (designed by the Art Nouveau painter Otto Gußmann) remained. The 98 m high tower, crowned by the golden figure of Hercules, is the highest in the town – one of the symbols of Dresden.

Cosel Palace

In 1744-46 the court-architect Johann Christoph Knöffel put up a palace for himself in the grounds of the old magazine; it was badly damaged when the Prussians fired on Dresden in 1760. Julius Heinrich Schwarze reconstructed and enlarged the palace in 1762-63 for Count Cosel, an illegitimate son of August the Strong. It was almost completely destroyed in 1945; until now only the two wings have been rebuilt.

Albertinum

It was built by Kaspar Voigt in 1559-63 (under Elector August) as an arsenal – a mighty four-wing building with a 75 m long double-nave columned hall, in which 600 battle and fortress guns were later stored. August the Strong's son had the building renovated and enlarged in 1740-47. The arsenal was no longer needed when the military barracks were put up in the Albertstadt. In 1884-87 Carl Adolf Canzler supervised the complete renovation, after which first the Saxon Main State Archive (1888) and then the Sculpture Collection (1894) were housed in the building. Partly destroyed in 1945, it was rebuilt in stages, and in 1964 opened up for the state art collections. At present it contains the Paintings Gallery (until 1992 also the Old Masters), the Green Vault, the Collection of Coins and Medals, the Sculpture Collection and important special exhibitions.

Art Academy and Art Society

Constantin Lipsius built the Art Academy on the Brühlsche Terrace in 1891-94 – in connection with the building of the Saxon Art Society – in the French baroque style. The glass dome with a bronze godess of victory by Robert Henze on the Art Society building is particularly striking. The people of Dresden call this dome the "lemon squeezer". Both buildings were considerably damaged during the war and have been only partly reconstructed. Today, the Art Academy houses the offices and departments of painting and graphic arts.

The Saxon Art Academy was founded as early as 1764; one of its first professors was Giovanni Battista Casanova, a brother of the famous adventurer. Later, artists such as Anton Graff, Ludwig Richter, Robert Sterl, Oskar Kokoschka and Otto Dix were active here. In 1990 the "New Saxon Art Society" was founded; one of its aims is the reconstruction of its old building.

Dome of the Art Society

Blockhaus ("Log Cabin")

At the Neustadt end of the Augustus Bridge there used to be a customs house which was taken down in 1727 and built up in 1732-53 to plans by Zacharias Longuelune as the Neustadt guard house. The somewhat misleading name "Log Cabin" derives from the previous wooden building. After being added to in 1892, it was for a time the seat of the Saxon war ministry. It was destroyed during the war and rebuilt as the 18th century original (1980). Now it functions as a concert hall and a restaurant.

Former Ministry of Finance

The building on the Neustadt bank of the Elbe, designed in late historical style by the architects Wanckel and Reichelt,was completed in 1896. The gable front facing the Elbe is remarkable: it shows an allegorical depiction of Saxonia on majolica tiles which the painter of historical scenes, Anton Dietrich, designed. The building is now used by the Saxon regional government.

Former General Ministry

The architects Waldow and Tscharmann built the General Ministry on the Neustadt bank of the Elbe in 1904-06; it is striking because of its wide tower. This, too, is in late historical style, its basic structure corresponding to the pattern of the palazzo. The building is used by the Saxon regional government.

County Court
Lothringer Str. I

This imposing four-wing building with corner towers and rough sandstone facade was planned by the architect Arwed Roßbach (1888-1892). He followed the Florentine renaissance architecture, adding baroque elements. The sculptural decoration on the porch is the work of the Dresden sculptor Johannes Schilling.

Marcolini Palace (Friedrichstadt Hospital)
Friedrichstraße

In about 1728 Johann Christoph Naumann began to build this castle for the Duchess of Teschen; after 1736 Johann Christoph Knöffel converted it into a country seat for Count Brühl. In 1774 the palace was taken over by Count Camillo Marcolini, who later had Johann Daniel Schade and J.Gottfried Kuntsch add the east wing. Napoleon stayed here in 1813, and Richard Wagner lived here in 1847-49 when working on "Lohengrin" and "Siegfried's Death".
The building has been used as a hospital since 1849. Dresden's most important fountain is located in the grounds: designed by Zacharias Longuelune, it was created by the sculptor Lorenzo Mattielli in 1744.

Castles on the Elbe
Bautzner Straße

Albrechtsberg Castle: Around 1850

Prince Albrecht, a brother of the Prussian king Friedrich Wilhelm IV, moved to Dresden, bought the land belonging to the Lord Findlater Vineyard between Dresden and Loschwitz, and had a castle built there from 1851 to 1854. The architect was a pupil of Schinkel's, Adolph Lohse, who drafted the plans for Albrechtsberg Castle in the tradition of Berlin Classicism. It is impressive how he included the slopes down to the river in the architecture of the castle grounds. From 1951 to 1989 the castle was used by the "Pioneers", the communist children's organization. Its future use is still being discussed – perhaps it will be turned into a European cultural centre.

Lingner Castle: At the same time as Albrechtsberg Castle, Adolph Lohse also built the neighbouring castle for Baron von Stockhausen, the prince's chamberlain; although it is smaller, it has the same characteristics. At the end of the 19th century it was purchased by Karl August Lingner, a factory owner who had become rich by inventing the mouthwash "Odol". When he died, he left it to the town of Dresden. Today it is the "Dresden Club", used for diverse functions.

Eckberg Castle: The most picturesque of the three castles on the Elbe was built in 1859-61 by the pupil of Semper, Christian Friedrich Arnold, in the English neo-Gothic style. It is one of the most beautiful and idyllic monuments to late Dresden Romanticism. Today it serves as an hotel.

Pillnitz Castle***
On the spot where the present New Palace stands there was originally a large late-renaissance four-wing

building, which Elector Johann Georg IV had given his mistress, Sibylle von Neitschütz. In 1706 August the Strong bought it back and in turn gave it to his mistress, Countess Cosel, a year later. However, when she fell out of favour, he dispossessed her of Pillnitz as well as Taschenberg Palace. The first plans for a pleasance were made in 1720. By 1724 Matthäus Daniel Pöppelmann had built the Water and Hill Palaces "in an oriental manner". The models for this unusual architecture were the pictures of temples and buildings on Chinese and Japanese porcelain. The wide, curved flight of steps from the Water Palace down to the river is particularly impressive. The castle was, from 1765 onwards, the permanent summer residence of the House of Wettin; so the first extensions (1788-91) became necessary – under the supervision of Christian Friedrich Exner to the designs by Christian Traugott Weinlig or Johann Daniel Schade.

Pillnitz, castle grounds

After the Old Palace had been destroyed by fire in 1818, Christian Friedrich Schuricht built the New Palace between 1822 and 1826, using classical elements that fitted in well. The hall in the middle wing is the only large room in Dresden that is decorated in the neoclassical style. Christian Vogel von Vogelstein did the murals and ceiling frescoes in this hall, as well as in the Catholic chapel. The Pillnitz grounds are almost unique in illustrating nearly the complete history of landscape gardening.

The French-style pleasance and hedge garden, as well as the Maillebahn, adjoins on the hilly side the English garden that was laid out in or about 1780. Finally, in the 19th century the landscape garden was created from a scientific viewpoint and planted with rare, exotic bushes and trees. The charm of this spacious park is increased by two pavilion buildings (the English Pavilion and the Chinese Pavilion), as well as the magnificent late 18th/early 19th century gondola in the hedge garden.

Churches

Cathedral, former Catholic Court Church***

This church is not only the most important point in the famous town silhouette of Dresden, it is now also the most significant sacred building, from the art-historical point of view, in the Saxon capital. After August the Strong had been converted in 1697, enabling him to become king of Catholic Poland, it was impossible to even think of building a prestigious Catholic church, for the Lutheran population of Saxony would have rebelled.

At first, the Catholic services were held in a modest chapel on the first floor of the Residence Castle, and then from 1707 onwards in the empty opera house adjoining the castle. August the Strong was little interested in religious matters. After his death,his son and successor August III devoted his attention to the building of a Catholic church. The Protestant town council had begun building the Church of Our Lady in 1726, which was to become the most important Lutheran sacred building in Europe; so it was for the Saxon Elector, who was at the same time king of Catholic Poland, not only a question of religious conviction but also a political necessity to erect a prestigious Catholic church within the Residence. After a long period of intensive and secret planning, the Roman master builder Gaetano Chiaveri was entrusted with the undertaking in 1737.

Chiaveri, who employed only Italian skilled workers, left Dresden again in 1743, so work on the building had to be continued by the German architects Sebastian Wetzel, Johann Christoph Knöffel and Julius Heinrich Schwarze. The church was consecrated in 1751 when still unfinished. When the building was completed in 1755, the total cost amounted to 1.041000 thalers. The Court Church was badly damaged on February 13th 1945. By 1979 most of it had been restored, but the complete restoration will take some more years.

Schilling, group of figures in front of the Court Church

The Court Church is a basilica with three naves and four corner chapels. The two-storey processional gallery round the nave was necessary because according to Roman Catholic rites all kinds of religious services were confined to the church building. As it had to be integrated into the urban surroundings, the church did without the usual east-west alignment. The 83.50 m high tower, divided into four storeys, is at the north-east end of the church, facing the Augustus Bridge. The 78 larger than lifesize sandstone statues by the Italian Lorenzo Matielli are particularly characteristic. In addition to Balthasar Permoser's late baroque pulpit (1722), the precious furnishings include the high altarpiece "The Ascension of Christ" by Anton Raphael Mengs (1751) and the organ,the greatest and last work of the famous organ builder Gottfried Silbermann. In 1973 a piéta of Meissen porcelain by the sculptor Friedrich Press was installed in the north-east chapel (formerly Nepomuk Chapel) – it is in memory of the "victims of the 13th of February 1945 and of all unjust violence". In the crypt there are the grand coffins of the Wettins, as well as a simple copper vessel on a bracket containing the heart of August the Strong, who was buried in Cracow. The Catholic Court Church, which was raised by Vatican decree to the Cathedral Sanctissimae Trinitatis of the Dresden/Meissen diocese in 1980, is considered to be one of the great achievements of Roman baroque art – of the highest European standard. (See Church Music)

The Church of Our Lady***

Dresden's oldest church "of Our Lady" stood from the 11th century onwards on the future Neumarkt. The building was altered several times and had to be torn down at the beginning of the 18th century, because it had become dilapidated and was too small for the increasing number of church-goers. In 1722 the Dresden official carpenter George Bähr was commissioned with the building of a new church. It was to have a square ground plan with bevelled corners, at which the four corner towers with the stairways inside were placed. There were five galleries spanned between the pillars. Above the magnificent, towering altar was the organ, made by the famous Gottfried Silbermann. The Protestant theory of church architecture had not been developed until the beginning of the 18th century; Bähr managed to apply this theory to his conception of the church in a unique way. The 95 m high dome, which dominated the town, was greatly admired – it was the first giant cupola made of stone in Europe since the ancient world. The Church of Our Lady was able to seat 4000 and was consecrated in 1738. During the Seven Years' War it survived the three-day bombardment by the Prussian troops without damage. The air raid on February 13th 1945 set it on fire: two days later it collapsed. The rebuilding of Dresden's best-known symbol was prevented by the communist town authorities. The impressive ruined building was later regarded as a reminder of the destruction of Dresden. Since 1982 members of peace and civil rights movements have gathered here each year on February 13th. Thus this church became a symbol of the peaceful protest of the people: it was one of the sources of the 1989 autumn revolution. On February 13th 1990 an "Initiative for the Rebuilding of the Church of Our Lady" appealed to the world with the following: "45 years after its destruction, the time has come for the Church of Our Lady to be rebuilt, as an obligation to and part of European culture".

Church of the Cross

The Church of the Cross was built from 1764 to 1792 to plans by Johann Georg Schmid and Christian Friedrich Exner. The architecture of this mighty sandstone building reflects the transition from the traditional Dresden baroque to classical design. The church has three predecessors, the earliest of which was put up at the beginning of the 13th century. The interior was several times damaged by fire and redecorated for the last time at the turn of the century – in a combination of neo-baroque and Art Nouveau.

After its destruction in 1945, the outer walls were restored, whereas the interior was left relatively unadorned; this emphasizes the hugeness of this hall with its 5000 seats and the scars of war. The Church of the Cross is the diocesan church of the Lutheran Church of Saxony and also the home of the world-famous choir. (See Church Music).

Semper Opera

Johanneum

Anna Church
Annenstr.

This church, dedicated to the Saxon Electoress Anna, was originally built in 1578 in renaissance style; destroyed by Prussian troups in 1760, it was reconstructed from 1764 to 1769 according to plans by Johann Georg Schmid in baroque style. The altar by the distinguished Saxon sculptor Hans Walther II originally belonged to the Church of the Cross which had burnt out in 1760 - here it was transformed into a pulpit altar. The Anna Church burnt out in 1945 and was rebuilt by 1950. The classical tower by the architect Gottlob Friedrich Thormeyer, however, is still lacking its helm roof. As well as for services, the church is also often used for concerts and lectures.

Epiphany Church**
Straße der Befreiung (Hauptstr.)

The Epiphany Church, the Neustadt parish church, has a Gothic predecessor, which was almost completely destroyed by the Hussites in 1429 and rebuilt in 1525. Old Dresden fell victim to a town fire in 1685, and with it this church. By 1691 it had been reconstructed, but a short time later it had to give way to the new main road (Straße der Befreiung), which was to become the most important axis of the meticulously planned new district of Neustadt. It was re-erected nearer to the street from 1732 to 1739 according to plans by George Bähr, the builder of the Church of Our Lady, and Matthäus Daniel Pöppelmann, the builder of the Zwinger.
The 87.50 m high tower on the west side was added in the middle of the 19th century. After its destruction during the war it is now being put up again – but the impressive hall of the church has been sacrificed: two thirds of the nave were divided off and now contain rooms on several floors which are used by the Saxon regional church. Until the historic Ständehaus has been rebuilt, the Saxon regional parliament has its sittings in a conference hall of the Epiphany Church.

Matthew Church
Friedrichstr.

The church is situated in Friedrichstadt; it was built from 1728 to 1730, probably to plans by Matthäus Daniel Pöppelmann who was buried here in 1736. The typically Protestant hall of the church with 2 galleries and a pulpit altar was destroyed in 1945 and rebuilt in 1974-78. Whereas the original style was kept to on the exterior, the interior is modern.

Russian-Orthodox Church
Juri-Gagarin-Str.

In the second half of the 19th century numerous foreigners settled in the exclusive residential areas to the east and south of the Main Station. They didn't integrate, the majority of the Dresdeners being Protestant; so between 1869 and 1884 four churches for foreigners were built.

The Anglican, American and Scottish-Presbyterian Churches were destroyed in 1945 – only the Russian-Orthodox Church remained standing. This picturesque sandstone building,with its 5 gilded onion-shaped domes, was consecrated in 1874 and served the large Russian colony, as well as the neighbouring embassy.

The main decoration in the church is the marble icon wall that separates the nave from the inner sanctum. The icons are the work of James Marshall, who also painted the auditorium ceiling in the Semper Opera.

Martin Luther Church
Martin-Luther-Platz

In 1883-87 the architects Ernst Giese and Paul Weidner built one of the most impressive 19th century churches in Dresden, situated on the outskirts of Neustadt which was at that time a new residential area. This basilica combines a Gothic basic form with Romanesque elements. The 81 m high tower certainly adds to the quality of the Dresden district of Neustadt.

Garrison Church
Dr.-Kurt-Fischer-Allee

The neo-Romanesque Garrison Church was built in Albertstadt, the Dresden garrison district, in 1897-1900. It was used by the members of the armed forces of both religious denominations. The Catholic part was restored after the war and is now a Catholic parish church; the Protestant part serves as a storeroom for books belonging to the Saxon regional library.

Christ Church**
Altstrehlen

Built by the architects Rudolf Schilling and Julius Gräbner in 1903-05, this was the first Art Nouveau church in Germany. It was completely renovated a few years ago.

It has retained most of the original decoration, which was the work of Dresden artists.

Loschwitz Church
Pillnitzer Landstr.

In 1705-1708 George Bähr and Johann Fehre the Elder built an octagonal church with garret roof and ridge turret in the former fishing village of Loschwitz. It was destroyed in 1945, although the Dresden district of Loschwitz remained almost completely untouched. For some time a citizens' action group has been campaigning for the rebuilding of this charming baroque village church.

Maria at the Water in Hosterwitz
Kirchgasse

This boatsmen's church right on the Elbe river dates back to the early 16th century; in 1704 it was renovated and enlarged. The baroque dome of the west tower was also added at this time. The attraction of the church lies particularly in the balance of its all-in-all simple architecture – and in its delightful surroundings on the Elbe. See Church Music.

Vineyard Church in Pillnitz

Matthäus Daniel Pöppelmann built this church in 1725 as a simple square building with wooden roof turrets. In spite of its simplicity, it is tremendously effective here in the lovely Pillnitz vineyards. After years of neglect an attempt is being made to use it for exhibitions and concerts.

Music and Theatre in Dresden

The Music Scene

Dresden's music tradition is unprecedented in Germany. For centuries the occupation with music was a matter of the court and the citizens: thus Dresden can pride itself on the world-famous Dresden State Orchestra, the former court orchestra of the Wettins, as well as the Philharmonic Orchestra of the town of Dresden. Both orchestras, whose members also play in numerous chamber music groups, give their concerts mainly in the hall of the Palace of Culture. Chamber concerts also take place in the German Hygiene Museum, the Country House (the Museum for the History of Dresden), the "Log Cabin", in the Porcelain Collection and in the Gobelin Hall in the Zwinger, which is still being restored. The serenades in front of the Water Palace at Pillnitz Castle are a particular attraction.
According to experts, Dresden audiences are well-informed, critical, but quick to show their enthusiasm. Among the stars in the Dresden music scene are the singers Peter Schreier, Theo Adam and Olaf Bär, the trumpeter Ludwig Güttler, the horn player Peter Damm and the harpist Jutta Zoff.

The furtherance of modern symphonic music is the aim of the Dresden centre of contemporary music, where concerts, symposiums and congresses take place.

The most important music event is the Dresden Music Festival, which takes place at the end of May and beginning of June each year; under the respective mottos there are numerous performances of music and music theatre.

Concert Halls

Kulturpalast
Altmarkt
8010 Dresden, Tel. 48660

Deutsches Hygienemuseum
Lingnerplatz 1
8010 Dresden, Tel. 4967219

Museum für die Geschichte der Stadt Dresden/Landhaus
Ernst-Thälmann-Str. 2
8010 Dresden, Tel. 4952302

Blockhaus
Neustädter Markt 19
8060 Dresden, Tel. 53630, 54421

Dresdner Klub
Bautzner Str. 132
8060 Dresden, Tel 54785

Porzellansammlung
Zwinger
8010 Dresden, Tel. 4840127

Carl-Maria-von-Weber-Gedenkstätte
Dresdner Str. 44
8054 Dresden, Tel. 39234

Dresdner Zentrum
für zeitgenössische Musik
Schevenstr. 17/150-95
8054 Dresden, Tel. 378281

The Theatre Scene

This is dominated by the music theatre with the world-famous opera. Heinrich Schütz, who was engaged as court director of music, composed "Daphne" here in 1627, the first German opera. There followed Carl Maria von Weber, Richard Wagner and Richard Strauss, most of whose works were performed for the first time in this magnificent building. Giuseppe Sinopoli will be musical director as from 1991.

In the last few years, the Dresden State Theatre, one of the DDR's most important theatres, has often had surprisingly sensational productions. As well as the churches, the Dresden theatres were often a podium for political discussions during the 1989 autumn revolution.

An increasing number of smaller and experimental theatres are also part of the Dresden theatre scene.

Theatres

Semper Opera
(Dresden State Opera)***
Theaterplatz 2
8010 Dresden, Tel. 48420,
evening box office: 4842491

In 1838-41 Gottfried Semper built his first opera house, which was soon, in 1869, destroyed by fire. Because Semper had taken part in the 1849 political disturbances, he had to leave Dresden. However, at the instigation of the citizens he was commissioned with the building of the new opera house, which was put up under the direction of his son in 1871-78.

This magnificently decorated building in high renaissance style is one of the most important 19th century theatres. Partly destroyed on February 13th 1945, it took several years to restore: 40 years to the day later this exact copy of the original was officially opened. Those who lack the time to go to the opera should at least take part in a guided tour of this impressive building.

State Operetta
Pirnaer Landstr. 131
8054 Dresden
Tel. advance booking: 4842351,
evening box office: 2238763

Schauspielhaus
Julian-Grimau-Allee
8010 Dresden, Tel. 48420,
evening box office: 4842429

Kleines Haus
Togliattistr. 28
8060 Dresden, Tel. 48420,
evening box office: 52631

Landesbühnen Sachsen
(opera and theatre)
Wilhelm-Pieck-Str. 152
8122 Radebeul Tel. 7040

Theater der Jungen Generation
(theatre for children and young people)
Meißner Landstr. 4
8029 Dresden, Tel. 437267

Studiotheater im Kulturpalast
Schloßstr.
8010 Dresden, Tel. 48660

Staatliches Puppentheater
(State Puppet Theatre)
Leipziger Str. 220
8030 Dresden, Tel. 51124, 570980

Dresdner Brettl
Maternistr. 17, PSF 462
8012 Dresden, Tel. 4954123

Podium
für Kunst, Körper,
Kommunikation
am Goldenen Reiter
Straße der Befreiung 11
8060 Dresden, Tel. 53266

Probebühne Astoria
Leipziger Str. 58
8023 Dresden

Schicht-Theater
im Kleinen Theater Reick
Reicker Str. 89
8036 Dresden, Tel. 48662, 472079

die bühne,
das kleine theater der tu
Teplitzer Str. 26
8020 Dresden, Tel. 4636351

Theater 50
Clara-Zetkin-Str. 44
8028 Dresden, Tel. 4327642

Kleine Szene
Bautzner Str. 107
8060 Dresden

Projekttheater Dresden
Luisenstr. 47
8060 Dresden

statt-theater Fassungslos
Elke Schubert
Bischofsweg 66
8060 Dresden

Dialog Theater
PSF 147
8027 Dresden

Open-air Theatres

"Junge Garde" im Großen Garten
8020 Dresden, Tel. 2391012

Parktheater am Palaisteich
Hauptallee
8010 Dresden

Puppentheater Sonnenhäusel
(puppet theatre)
Herkulesallee 1
8019 Dresden, Tel. 4594006

Konzertplatz Weißer Hirsch
8051 Dresden, Tel. 36115

Felsenbühne Rathen
(natural mountain stage)
8324 Rathen (see Landesbühnen Sachsen)
This open-air theatre, in a romantic rocky valley in "Saxon Switzerland", is one of the most beautiful in Europe. During the summer months various Saxon ensembles put on popular plays (for example, after Karl May), operettas and operas.

Church Music

Dresden is the most important centre of church music on the territory of the former DDR. The Kreuzchor (choir of the Church of the Cross), which has existed for 750 years, is one of the most renowned boys'

choirs in Europe. Its main task is the participation in services in the Church of the Cross. Evensong with choir or organ is held every Sunday at 6 pm.
The great Bach oratorio concerts, in which the Church of the Cross choir is accompanied by the Philharmonic or State Orchestra, are permanently sold out. At 6 o'clock in the morning on December 25th the choir performs its famous "nativity play". For many Dresdeners this is the highlight of the Christmas season. The "Dresden Requiem" is often on the programme on February the 13th – a shattering choral work that the former choirmaster Rudolf Mauersberger composed in 1945 when still stirred by the destruction of Dresden. The choir's counterpart is that of the Catholic Court Church, which has left its mark there for more than 2 centuries. As opposed to the Church of the Cross choir, it is devoted entirely to sacral music and is thus, in spite of its excellent musical qualities, not as well-known. It is well worth going to hear the choir when it sings one of the great Masses in the Cathedral. The concerts which the choir of the school of church music gives from time to time in the different Dresden churches are also first-class. Especially at Christmas time and in Lent, oratorios are performed in several Dresden churches (including the Versöhnungskirche Strießen, Diakonissenhauskirche, Lukaskirche, Christuskirche Strehlen, Markuskirche Pieschen).
An essential part of church music in the town are the organ services which take place in the Cathedral during the summer months every Saturday at 4 p.m. The big organ in the Church of the Cross, which was built by the Dresden firm Jehmlich in 1963, can be heard at the Saturday evening service at 6 p.m. In addition to this, organ concerts are also given in the following churches: Petrikirche, Auferstehungskirche, Markuskirche, Martin-Luther-Kirche, Diakonissenhauskirche and Maria am Wasser in Hosterwitz. Information on the wide choice of church music events is given by poster advertising and the Dresden press.

Jazz and Rock Music

Dixieland is dominating in the Dresden jazz scene. The highlight each year is the international Dixieland Festival at the beginning of May, which is celebrated like a public festival. You can hear good jazz of a quite different kind in various clubs, where singer-songwriters and rock bands perform. During the summer months there are large open-air concerts, including ones on the open-air stage "Junge Garde". But the future of the usual park festival in August, with numerous big rock concerts, is at the moment uncertain – due to financial difficulties.

Clubs

Jazz Klub "Tonne"
Tzschirnerplatz 3
8010 Dresden, Tel. 4951354
The most important Dresden jazz club is located in the barrel vaulting in the ruins of the Kurländer Palace, which was destroyed in 1945.

Students' Club "Bärenzwinger"
Brühlscher Garten
8010 Dresden, Tel. 4951104, 4634699
This has been a popular students' club since the 1960's; it is in the vaults just down from the Brühlsche Terrace, roughly on the spot where Böttger invented Meissen porcelain.

"Scheune" central youth club
Allaunstr. 36/40
8060 Dresden, Tel. 55532

Students' club "Spirale"
Nöthnitzer Str. 46
8027 Dresden, Tel. 4636038

Notenkeller
Fritz-Heckert-Platz 13
8010 Dresden, Tel. 4590213

Students' club of the University of Art WENDEL
Terrassengasse
8010 Dresden, Tel. 4952457
Thurs. 8 p.m. - 1 a.m.

Youth club house "Rudi Arndt"
Fechnerstr. 2a
8030 Dresden, Tel. 5692883

Smaller Museums and Memorials

Museum of Early
Dresden Romanticism
Straße der Befreiung 13
8060 Dresden, Tel. 54760
Closed on Mondays and Tuesdays
The exhibition is in the house belonging to the painter Gerhard von Kügelgen, which was built in the 17th century; it contains arts and crafts giving information on early Dresden Romanticism in literature, the fine arts and music.

Schiller House
Schillerstr. 19
8054 Dresden
The Körner family's former garden house was where Schiller worked on "Don Carlos". He also wrote "Ode to Joy" here. The house contains contemporary furniture and keepsakes from Schiller's years in Dresden.

Jozef Ignacy Kraszewski Museum
Nordstr. 28
8060 Dresden, Tel. 573171
Closed on Mondays and Tuesdays and during the winter months.
The popular Polish poet, who emigrated to Dresden after participating in the 1830-31 rebellion in Warsaw, lived in this idyllically situated villa for several years; it now houses a delightful museum which deals with, in addition to Kraszewski, numerous Polish emigrants living in Dresden in the 19th century.

Carl Maria von Weber Memorial*
Dresdner Str. 44
8057 Dresden, Tel. 39234
Closed on Mondays and Tuesdays
This former wine-grower's house served as the Weber family's summer house from 1818 to 1824: essential parts of "Freischütz" and the "Invitation to Dance" were composed here. Numerous possessions of Weber's help to give information on his life and work. Concerts are given here occasionally.

Richard Wagner Museum Graupa*
Richard-Wagner-Str. 6
8304 Graupa, Tel. Pirna 3437
Closed on Fridays and Saturdays
Wagner spent some time in this village, not far from Dresden, during the summer of 1846, in order to start work on "Lohengrin" in peace and quiet. The farmhouse he lived in at that time is now the only Wagner museum on the territory of the former DDR. An exhibition is devoted to "Richard Wagner and Dresden". Concerts and lectures take place here from time to time.

Martin Andersen Nexö Memorial
Collenbuschstr. 4
8051 Dresden, Tel. 36307
Closed on Thursdays and Fridays and during the winter months.
The Danish poet Martin Andersen Nexö spent his last years here in this villa. This small museum includes an exhibition,on the ground floor, on the poet's life and work, and his study on the 1st floor which has remained unchanged.

Memorial in the Georg Schumann Building of the Technical University
Salvador-Allende-Platz 1
8027 Dresden, Tel. 4634005
Open daily.
In this former regional court building there used to be a prison with a total of 700 cells. About 1000 opponents of the National Socialist regime were beheaded here between 1939 and 1945. In 1990 it became known that death sentences were carried out after 1945 as well. The SED (Communist Party) did not only have former Nazi functionaries executed here, but also its own political opponents. The death cells have been kept in their original condition.

Carl Maria von Weber

Monuments to the History of Technology and Transport

The White Fleet*

The famous paddle-steamers, some of which are over a hundred years old, are still in use, flying the flag of the Dresden shipping company. The engine-room usually has a glass cover, so that the passengers can watch the steam-engine with its shining pistons and shafts from above. The showpiece of the fleet is the "Diesbar" which was built in 1846 and recently restored true to the original. In the 2nd class saloon there is a small exhibition on steam navigation on the Upper Elbe. The luxurious 1st class saloon is now a restaurant. When the steamer is not in use, it is berthed at the Terrassenufer and can be visited. From April until October the steamers and motor vessels of the White Fleet go up the Elbe to the Sandstone Hills and down the Elbe to Meissen and Riesa. There are also special trips to Czechoslovakia. The connection to Hamburg was opened up again recently.

Funicular Railway Loschwitz-Bad Weißer Hirsch

The cable railway was built in 1895; it takes 4.5 minutes to cover a distance of 547 m and a difference in altitude of 95 m. It was originally operated by steam, then in 1905 converted to electricity. Both the counter-balanced cabins pass through two tunnels on their way to the station at the top, which is right next to the popular restauant "Luisenhof".

Cable Railway Loschwitz-Oberloschwitz

It was put into service in 1901 as the first passenger cable car railway in the world. It takes three minutes to cover an altitude of 84 m on a 280 m stretch. Although it is a normal transport connection with Oberloschwitz, it is mainly a tourist attraction. After many years of restoration and general repair, the line will be re-opened in 1991.

Park Railway

During the 1930's there was a park railway on the Exhibition Grounds in the Large Garden. The idea was taken up again after the war and the Pioneers' Railway opened in 1950. The open trains, which are pulled by little steam or electric engines, cover a distance of 5.1 km with 4 stations. The railway was looked after by the Pioneers, members of the communist children's organization. After the "change" in 1990 the name was altered to Park Railway; it is still an attraction, not only for children.

Traditional Railway Radebeul/East-Radeburg*

The narrow-gauge railway (750mm gauge) was built in 1884 and is registered as a technical monument. It runs through the delightful Lößnitz vineyard countryside and the Moritzburg lake area up to Radeburg, a small town 16.5 km away from Radebeul. A saloon coach can be hired for celebrations. The journeys with the original coaches of the Royal Saxon State Railway are a special attraction: the passengers wear costumes dating back to the turn of the century.

Narrow-Gauge Railway Freital/Hainsberg-Kipsdorf

Little puffing steam engines pull the trains on this narrow-gauge railway, which has been in use since 1882. It runs through the lovely countryside of the Plauenscher Grund to Kipsdorf, a popular place for outings in the eastern Erzgebirge (Ore-Mountains).

Yenidze

The cigarette factory, which was built in 1907 in the shape of a mosque, is probably the strangest edifice in the Saxon capital. The glass dome, which is illuminated at night, was supposed to convey oriental associations – an advertisment for the famous "oriental cigarettes". The Yenidze can certainly be counted as a monument of industrial architecture; today it is a branch office of a tobacco firm.

Blue Miracle*

The bridge was a world sensation when it was officially opened in 1893, after taking three years to build. Because it was painted blue, people soon called it "The Blue Miracle". Claus Köpcke and Hans Manfred Krüger designed the suspension bridge, which spans the Elbe River without pylons over a length of 141.5 metres. In 1945 it was the only bridge to remain intact: two Dresden citizens, independent of one another, had cut the explosion wire that the SS had laid. This Blue Miracle is a technical construction that harmonizes well with the surrounding built-up area.
The aesthetic charm of the filigree of its iron construction made the Blue Miracle into one of the best-known symbols of Dresden.

Monuments

Moritz Monument by Hans Walther, 1553, Brühlsche Terrasse

Equestrian statue of August the Strong, model by J.J. Vinache, coppersmith L. Wiedemann, 1732, Neustadt Market – one of Dresden's symbols.

General Moreau Monument
by G.F. Thormeyer and G.C. Kühn, 1814, Räcknitzhöhe

Monument King Friedrich August the Just, by Ernst Rietschel, 1843, Karl Marx Platz

Carl Maria von Weber, by Ernst Rietschel, 1860, between the Opera and the Paintings Gallery

Electoress Anna, by Robert Henze, 1869, at the Anna Cemetery

Theodor Körner, by Julius Hähnel,

Loschwitz, “Blue Miracle”

Albrechtsberg Castle

1871, Leningrader Str. corner Bürgerwiese

Ernst Rietschel, by Johannes Schilling, 1872, Brühlsche Terrasse

King Friedrich August II, by Julius Hähnel, 1877, Neumarkt

Gustav Nieritz, by Gustav Kietz, 1878, Dr.-Conert-Str.

Martin Luther, by Adolf Donndorf and Ernst Rietschel, 1885, in front of the ruins of the Church of Our Lady

Equestrian statue King Johann, by Johannes Schilling, 1889, Castle Square

Gottfried Semper, by Johannes Schilling, 1892, Brühlsche Terrasse

Emperor Wilhelm I and King Albert, by Karl Heinrich Epler, 1893, flagpoles on the Neustadt Market

Friedrich Schiller, by Selmar Werner, 1913, Hauptstraße (Str. der Befreiung)

Schiller Körner Monument, by Oskar Rassau, 1913, Schillerstraße Loschwitz

Soviet Memorial, by O. Rost, 1945, Platz der Einheit

Woman who Clears away Rubble after Bombing, by W. Reinhold, 1953, New Town Hall

Lenin Memorial, by G. Jastrebenezki, 1974, Wiener Platz

Johann Friedrich Böttger, by Peter Makolies, 1982, Brühlsche Terrasse

Caspar David Friedrich, by Eike Kutschke, 1988, Brühlsche Terrasse

It is at present uncertain what will happen with the post-war monuments that are devoted to political subjects. But the Lenin Monument will certainly be pulled down.

Cemeteries

Elias Cemetery
Güntzplatz
The plague cemetery was consecrated in 1680 and became an important burial ground in the 18th century with many artistically significant tombstones, of which several were designed by Caspar David Friedrich. Here lie among others, the archaeologist Carl August Böttiger (1760-1835), the famous Norwegian landscape painter Johann Christian Clausen Dahl (1788-1857) and the architect Gottlob Friedrich Thormeyer (1778-1842). The cemetery was closed in 1945 and has since become a wilderness; however, thought is being given to the restauration of this interesting cemetery.

The Inner Catholic Cemetery
Friedrichstraße
In 1721 August the Strong consecrated this cemetery for his Habsburg daughter-in-law Maria Josepha; however, it soon afterwards served as the cemetery for the citizens of the Residence of Catholic belief and of many Italians who, as artists and artisans, helped to build up Dresden. In the 19th century many Polish emigrants found their last resting place

here. A great number of graves in baroque, rococo and neoclassic style are also in this cemetery. Here are also the Crucifixion figures Balthasar Permoser (1651-1732) created for his own grave, and the last resting place of Carl Maria von Weber (1786-1826) which was the work of Gottfried Semper. Among others are: Giovanni Batista Casanova (1730-1795), the brother of the well-known adventurer, who served as Director of the Academy in Dresden, the sculptor Ernst Julius Hähnel (1811-1891), the painter Gerhard von Kügelgen (1772-1820), and the writers Friedrich Schlegel (1772-1829) and Ludwig Tieck (1773-1853).

The Outer Catholic Cemetery
Bremer Straße
In the second Catholic cemetery, consecrated in 1875, lies the grave of the famous Romantic painter Ludwig Richter (1803-1884).

The Matthäus Cemetery
Friedrichstraße
Near to the Inner Catholic Cemetery is the Protestant cemetery, consecrated in 1725. In the adjoining Matthäus Church is the tomb of the builder of the Zwinger, Matthäus Daniel Pöppelmann (1662-1736). In the cemetery itself are buried, among others, the designer of the first German steam locomotive, Johann Andreas Schubert (1808-1870), and the painter Wilhelm Walther (1826-1913), who created the "Fürstenzug" ("Parade of Princes").

The Inner Neustadt Cemetery
Conradstraße
This cemetery, consecrated in 1731 and replacing the old Epiphany Churchyard, has many significant tombs of the 18th and 19th centuries. The sculptor Gottfried Knöffler (1715-1779), the writer Elisabeth von der Recke (1756-1833) and the poet Christian August Tiedge (1752-1841) are buried here.

Trinitatis Cemetery
Fiedlerstraße
Following an epidemic – a new cemetery was necessary. In 1815 it was consecrated and in ensuing years several times enlarged. The visioned concept was designed by the architect Gottlob Friedrich Thormeyer, by whom is also the neoclassical tomb for the Russian general Michel de Habbe. A ten metre high obelisk commemorates the victims of the Dresden May Rebellion in 1849. Several of the tombs are works by Caspar David Friedrich and Ernst Rietschel – both buried here. Among others, the doctor, painter and philosopher Carl Gustav Carus (1789-1869), the librettist of "Freischütz" Friedrich Kind (1768-1843), the artist Ferdinand von Rayski (1806-1890), the actress Wilhelmine Schröder-Devrient (1804-1860) and the father of Clara Schumann, Friedrich Wieck (1785-1873) lie here.

Johannis Cemetery
Wehlener Straße
In the cemetery planned in 1881 on the Tolkewitz bank of the Elbe, lie, among others, the painter Ferdinand Dorsch (1875-1938) and Friedrich Preller jun. (1838-1901), as well as the famous art historian Cornelius Gurlitt (1850-1938).

The Urn Grove of the Crematorium
Wehlener Straße
Directly next to the Johannis Cemetery is the Crematorium, designed by Fritz Schumacher 1909-1911, which counts as one of the most impressive Art Nouveau buildings in Germany. It is surrounded by an urn grove, in which the painter Gotthard Kuehl (1851-1915) and the art historian Karl Woermann (1844-1933) are buried.

Loschwitz Cemetery
Pillnitzer Landstraße
Lying beneath the former royal vineyards on the banks of the Elbe is the idyllic old village cemetery which has been, since the beginning of the century, a preferential burial ground for Dresden's painters. Here lie, among others, Sascha Schneider, Hans Unger, Oskar Zwintscher, Josef Hegenbarth, Hans-Theo Richter, Ernst Hassebrauk, Willy Wolff and Hermann Glöckner.

Heide Cemetery
Moritzburger Landstraße
In the town cemetery (1929-1934) is

a mass grave for 30.000 victims of the bombing attack on February 13th 1945. Memorials remind one of the shelling of Dresden as well as the destruction of many other European cities – and of the victims of the National Socialist concentration camps. In and after 1945 Dresden's Communist Party prominent figures were buried here. In this cemetery is the tomb of the painter Hans Grundig (1901-1958).

Old Israelite Cemetery
Pulsnitzer Straße
For many years Dresden's Jews were obliged to bury their dead outside of Saxony. In 1751 permission was granted for a cemetery of their own. Overgrown rows of graves lie between huge linden and oak trees; the charm of this cemetery is in its simplicity and the thrifty use of decorative elements. The cemetery was closed in 1869, but may be visited after making an appointment with the Jewish Congregation (Bautzner Str. 8060 Dresden).

New Israelite Cemetery
Fiedlerstraße
As a replacement for the completely full-up Old Cemetery, a new Jewish cemetery was consecrated directly next to the Trinitatis cemetery. The cemetery chapel now serves the small Jewish community as a synagogue. The original Dresden synagogue, which Gottfried Semper had built on the Gondelhafen in 1838-40, was destroyed by the National Socialists on November 9th 1938.

Hotels and Guest-houses

Since the tourist business was greatly neglected during the DDR era, there is now a large deficit in the catering industry. Although two luxury hotels were built in the 1980's which could meet more sophisticated demands, still hotels of the better middle class are needed. Definitely there will be a vast improvement as far as the hotel and guest-house industry is concerned within the next few years.

Hotel Bellevue (Luxury class)

Köpckestraße 15, 8060 Dresden
Tel. 56620, Telefax 114143
This house, which can be counted as one of the most beautiful in Europe, offers a special flair in its combination of a baroque residence with double courtyard and the hotel annex built in 1985. The affluent guest finds here the luxury he may expect in this price category. The panoramic view of the Dresden town silhouette, which one can enjoy from the rooms facing towards the Elbe and from the restaurants, is particularly delightful. There is also a casino in the hotel.

Hotel Dresdner Hof (Luxury class)
An der Frauenkirche 5, 8010 Dresden
Tel. 20920, Telefax 114143
Opened in 1990, this luxury hotel is situated in the middle of the historic city centre. Via a covered bridge one reaches the Secundo Genitur, a baroque palace directly on the Brühlsche Terrasse, in which there is a café. All in all this hotel contains 15 restaurants, cafés and bars.

Hotel Newa (Good middle-class)
Leningrader Straße 34, 8010 Dresden
Tel. 496271, Telex 26067
This hotel, which is close to the Main Station, has its entrance on the Prager Straße; it was opened in the 1970's.

Hotel Astoria (Good middle-class)
Ernst-Thälmann-Platz 1,
8020 Dresden,
Tel. 44171, Telex 2442
This well-run hotel in a relatively quiet location (not far from the Large Garden) has been frequented for decades by artists.

Hotel Gewandhaus (middle-class)
Ringstraße 1, 8010 Dresden
Tel, 496286, Telex 2527
In the historic building of the Neue Gewandhaus an hotel was opened after the reconstruction in 1966, offering the advantage of a central location in the inner city.

Hotel Königstein and Hotel Lilienstein
Prager Straße, 8010 Dresden
Tel. 48560, Telex 2221
These two average middle-class hotels lie directly on the Prager Straße, which, as a pedestrian precinct, joins the Main Station to the Altmarkt.

Hotel Stadt Rendsburg (middle-class)
Kamenzer Straße 1, Tel. 51551
This well-run establishment, which offers at least some comfortable rooms, lies in the outer part of Neustadt, a somewhat derelict but nevertheless interesting quarter of the industrial period. Those who wish to get to know the Dresden scene have an ideal starting point here.

Hotel Rothenburger Hof
(Lower middle-class)
Rothenburger Straße 15-17,
8060 Dresden, Tel. 54269
This one too, lying on a busy street, belongs to the outer part of Neustadt.

Hotel Schloß Eckberg (middle-class)
Bautzner Straße 134, 8060 Dresden
In this attractive neo-Gothic castle, which is very pleasantly situated on the banks of the Elbe, a youth hostel was opened a couple of years ago. Meanwhile it is open to all.

Waldparkhotel (middle-class)
Prellerstr. 16, 8053 Dresden
Tel. 34441
This hotel lies within the residential area of Blasewitz, not far from the Schillerplatz.

Parkhotel Weißer Hirsch
(Low standard)
Bautzner Landstraße 7, Dresden
Tel. 36851 or 36852
This hotel is something for those with a certain inclination to nostalgia and asceticism. One sees that this hotel originated during the great time when the district Bad Weißer Hirsch was a spa of world renown. However, the onetime glory has rather faded...

To those who do not mind going without a toilet in the room, bath or shower, the traditional guest-houses on the Weißer Hirsch are to be recommended. Built for the spa guests of the that-time renowned Lahmann Sanatorium around the turn of the century, they have retained their somewhat morbid charm. One advantage is the quiet location in a pleasant villa quarter dating back to the turn of the century and the Waldpark in the Dresden Heide is quite near.

Pension Sonneneck
Plattleite 43, 8051 Dresden
Tel. 36430
In good weather one can have breakfast in a well-kept garden next to a splashing fountain.

Pension Geier
Plattleite 45, 8051 Dresden
Tel. 36483

Pension Steiner
Plattleite 49, 8051 Dresden
Tel. 36205

Fremdenheim Haus Roseneck
Plattleite 64, 8051 Dresden
Tel. 36140

Pension Monika
Plattleite 62, 8051 Dresden
Tel. 36132

Hotel Felsenburg
Rißweg 68, 8051 Dresden
Tel. 36664
Oskar Kokoschka, who lived for many years in this once artists' guest-house, called it "my rock castle" and wrote here his expressionist drama "Murderer, Hope of Women". Today the building looks somewhat derelict from the outside, like a bewitched castle. The interior has hardly changed since Kokoschka's time.

From Kitchen and Cellar

Cooking is not an occupation. Cooking is an art. And there are many who say that the Saxons were never good at it. Thus bemoaned the writer Johann Caspar Riesbeck, who travelled the whole of Germany in the 18th century and praised Saxony's culture but despised its kitchen. Is this predudice or truth? Those who have tasted Dresden cooking during the past 40 years are rather inclined to believe the latter. Looking deeper into the matter, studying old cookery books and talking to ambitious chefs, one is surprised to find a totally different situation. 40 years of "going without" and state control, with the famous standard menu between Cape Arkona and Zinnwald, were responsible for the fact that Saxon cooking developed into a terra incognita. Now Dresden's ambitious landlords and chefs are trying more and more to prove the identity of their kitchens. Long-since forgotten dishes are being rediscovered and make promise to Germany's gourmets that they have something to look forward to: the rediscovery of Saxony as a culinary landscape. Dresden cooking is hearty, is not afraid of "sweet-sour" but also knows subtle flavours. The Saxon potato salad is famous and is served in countless variations. Among the many items which are to be found more and more on Dresden menus are e.g.: Saxon boiled beef with raisins, tongue in raisin sauce, Dresden steak in onion sauce, Oldsaxon porkbelly and Dresden braised beef marinaded in vinegar. The defty Lausitz kitchen is also tasty and is served in many Dresden restaurants. Far superior to the Dresden beer is the spicy Radeberg Beer, brewed in a small town not far from Dresden.

A surprise of a special nature awaits the wine connoisseur, for who would have known that Europe's smallest and most northerly vineyards lie between Dresden and Meissen? Up to now it has been practically impossible to get the Elbe Valley wine, as the wine-growers had to cater for the needs of the Party and the government. Now one can find it on a few Dresden wine-cards. Experts praise the dry Elbe Valley wine as being full, pure and much stronger than those of comparable west-German vineyards.

Saxons' preference for coffee is proverbial. No less popular are all kinds of cakes and pastry. We can strongly recommend e.g. the "Dresdner Eierschecke", a light yeast-cottage-cheese cake, and "Pfefferkuchen" (peppernuts) from Pulsnítz. No recommendation is needed for the world-famous "Dresdner Christstollen". Year after year, during the Christmas season, it is not only produced by bakeries but also by housewives, each having their own special, "secret" recipe. This is the jewel of the Saxon art of baking.

Restaurants

The bombing attack in 1945 destroyed practically all of Dresden's historic inns. Most of the restaurants which were put up in the post-war years were tasteless and sterile. In the 1970's an attempt was made to open up some restaurants conveying the typical Dresden atmosphere, such as those on the "Straße der Befreiung".

Gastronomy in Dresden is still plagued by the heritage of the former DDR era. This applies not only to the appearance of the restaurants, but also to the quality of the food and service. Such obvious things as attractively designed menus and the serving of different dishes at the same time are rarely cared about. As a consequence of the social and financial burdens placed upon the former DDR citizens by the change to the free market and the currency reform, the inns are far less frequented than was previously the case. The prices were in many instances raised to the level of the former West Germany. This is why it is no problem to find a seat, even in popular restaurants for which one previously had to book months in advance. This situation leads to competition, which is very positive for the gastronomy as a whole. Even the most grumpy waiter must realize that he can only keep his job if he adopts the motto "service with a smile". At the same time many new restaurants are being established which try to keep high standards from the start.

There is, therefore, a noticeable trend towards improvemnent in Dresden's gastronomy. In order to avoid the inconvenience caused by the bad habit of constantly changing closing days, the telephone numbers are quoted.

City Restaurants

Altstadt side

Restaurant Leningrad
in the Newa Hotel
Leningrader. Str., 8010 Dresden
Tel. 4967112

Bistro de Saxe
in the Hotel Dresdner Hof
An der Frauenkirche 5, 8010 Dresden
Tel. 4841776

Restaurant International
Prager Str., Dresden
Tel. 4952565

Speisebar in the Café Prag
Altmarkt 16/17, 8010 Dresden
Tel. 4951135

Opera Restaurant
Theaterplatz 2, 8010 Dresden
Tel. 4842500
- quite good cooking - in good weather tables outside directly next to the Zwinger Lake

Kulturpalast Am Altmarkt
8010 Dresden, Tel. 4866306

Ratskeller
Dr.-Külz-Ring 19, Dresden
Tel. 4952581

Altmarktkeller
Ernst-Thälmann-Str. 19-21, Dresden
Tel. 4951212

Am Gewandhaus
Gewandhausstr. 3-7, 8010 Dresden
Tel. 4952342

Neustadt side

Palaisrestaurant
and Restaurant Elbterrasse
in the Hotel Bellevue
Köpckestr. 15, 8060 Dresden
Tel. 53425
– excellent cooking – view of the famous silhouette of the town

Blockhaus
Neustädter Markt 19, 8060 Dresden
Tel. 53 630
– view of the Altstadt and the Neustadt Markt

Kügelgenhaus and Neustädter Grill
Straße der Befreiung 13,
8060 Dresden,
Tel. 52791
– good dining restaurants with typical Dresden atmosphere

Gin-Gin
Straße der Einheit 29, 8060 Dresden
Tel. 53572

Piccolo, Friedrich-Engels-Str. 26,
8060 Dresden
Tel. 53168

Speciality Restaurants

Äberlausitzer Töppel
Straße der Befreiung 14, Dresden
Tel. 55605
– Saxon, Upper Lausitz cooking, Eibau dark beer

Restaurant Canaletto
in Hotel Bellevue
Köpckestr. 15, 8060 Dresden
Tel. 53425
– French cooking

Restaurant Le Gourmet
in the Hotel Dresdner Hof
An der Frauenkirche 5,
8010 Dresden
Tel. 4841776
– French cooking

Ristorante Rossini
in the Hotel Dresdner Hof
An der Frauenkirche 5,
8010 Dresden
Tel. 4841776
– Italian cooking

Pizza & Pasta
Bautzner Str., 8060 Dresden
– Italian cooking

Zichis Pizzeria
Hauptstr. 27, 8080 Dresden
Tel. 584570
– Italian cooking, pizzas from ovens using beech wood

Szeged
Ernst-Thälmann-Str. 4-6,
8010 Dresden,
Tel. 4951371
– Hungarian cooking, after 6pm with original gypsy music

Ostrawa
Fetscherstr. 30, 8019 Dresden
Tel. 4593131
– Bohemian cooking, Czech beer

Wrozlaw
Prager Str., 8010 Dresden
Tel. 4952565
– Polish cooking

Restaurant Buri-Buri
in the Hotel Bellevue
Köpckestr. 15, 8060 Dresden
Tel. 53425
– Polynesian cooking

Beer Restaurants

Bierclub No. 15
in the Hotel Bellevue
Köpckestr. 15, 8060 Dresden
Tel. 53425
– This beer restaurant is in the cellars of the baroque house, which is combined well with the new hotel building; it keeps numerous German and foreign brands of beer, including the best ones of the former DDR (Wernersgrüner, Radeberger, Urkrostitzer and Sternburg).

Bierkeller im Kügelgenhaus
Straße der Befreiung 13,
8060 Dresden
Tel. 52791
– Weapons, uniforms and historic etchings on the walls remind us of the wars of liberation. Dresden beer is served on wooden tables that have been cleaned until they shine.

Bierhaus Dampfschiff
in the Dresdner Hof
An der Frauenkirche 5, 8010 Dresden
Tel. 4841776
– wide choice of different kinds of beer

Radeberger Keller
Ernst-Thälmann-Str. 24,
8010 Dresden, Tel. 4951281
– Only Radeberg brands of beer are served here. Meat from their own slaughtering. It is not very fine here, but it is loud and informal.

Am Thor
Straße der Befreiung 37,
8060 Dresden, Tel. 51372

– a cosy beer bar on Dresden's nicest pedestrian precinct

Neustädter Faß
Leipziger Str. 28, 8023 Dresden
Tel. 574882
– This is mainly frequented by local people; you soon get talking with them when drinking good beer.

Wine Restaurants

Meißner Weinkeller
Straße der Befreiung 1b,
8060 Dresden,
Tel. 5555814
– Dresden's best wine restaurant is in the cellar of the Neustadt Town Hall, which was destroyed in 1945 and later torn down. In addition to various German and foreign wines, it serves all the available Elbe Valley wines.

Wackerbarths Keller
in Hotel Bellevue
Köpckestr. 15, 8060 Dresden
Tel. 53425
– exclusive wine restaurant with specifically Saxon atmosphere, including Meissen wines

Wettiner Keller in the Dresdner Hof
An der Frauenkirche 5, 8010 Dresden
Tel. 4841776
– elegant wine restaurant with Dresden flair and Meissen wines

Weinrestaurant Bacchus
Clara-Zetkin-Str. 15, 8028 Dresden
Tel. 4327996
– wine-tastings if ordered in advance

Weinrestaurant Laterne
Platz der Einheit, 8060 Dresden
Tel. 53094
– This restaurant is in the upper part of a new residential building; its advantages are the wide choice of wines and, above all, the fantastic view of the Platz der Einheit and the Straße der Befreiung, right over to the Altstadt bank of the Elbe.

Weinstube Rebstock
Niederwaldstr. 10, 8019 Dresden
Tel. 35350
– a popular, traditional Dresden restaurant

Basteischlößchen
Packhofstr., 8010 Dresden
– a small, elegant wine restaurant directly on the Altstadt bank of the Elbe. The terrace is open in good weather.

Altdresdner Winzerstube
Antonstr. 19, 8060 Dresden
Tel. 54113
– This is the meeting place for Dresden painters, art students, unrecognized authors and professional drinkers.

Recommended Restaurants in the Outlying Districts

Altstadt Side

Hotel Astoria
Ernst-Thälmann-Platz 1,
8020 Dresden
Tel. 475171
– good cooking

Borsbergeck
Borsbergstr. 31, 8019 Dresden
Tel. 35486
– good value

Hasenschenke
Bärensteinerstr. 13, 8021 Dresden
Tel. 38784
– popular restaurant for families

Gust'l Eck
Jacobistr. 9, 8019 Dresden
Tel. 35472
– cosy pub on the corner with good cooking

Augsburger Hof
Augsburger Str. 49, 8019 Dresden
Tel. 30667
– cosy beer pub

Maygarten Linie 6
Schaufußstr. 24, 8021 Dresden
Tel. 30268
– All the fittings are parts of old trams. The landlord occasionally tries his hand at a rather lewd kind of cabaret.

Neustadt Side

Drachenschenke

Bautzner Straße 72, 8060 Dresden
Tel. 51188
– historic restaurant directly on the Elbe

Luisenhof
Bergbahnstr. 8, 8051 Dresden
Tel. 36842
– This popular restaurant, called "Dresden's Balcony", is to be recommended especially for the view of the town and the Elbe Valley.

Restaurant Erholung, Weißer Hirsch
Rißweg 39, 8051 Dresden
Tel. 377993
– Everything about this small restaurant, one of the best in Dresden, is reminiscent of the hey-day of the now town district Bad Weißer Hirsch; at the beginning of the century it was a world-famous health resort. In order to recover from the meagre diet in the renowned Lahmann Sanatorium, many–including Marikka Rökk, Theo Lingen and Paul Lincke – stopped off at the "Erholung", which has existed since 1861. Today it serves international cooking of quite good quality.

Trompeter
Bautzner Landstr. 83, 8051 Dresden
Tel. 36123
– historic restaurant at the edge of the Dresden Heide.

Hubertusgarten
Bautzner Landstr. 89, 8051 Dresden
Tel. 36074
– historic game restaurant at the edge of the Dresden Heide.

Körnergarten
Friedrich-Wieck-Str. 26,
8054 Dresden
Tel. 36620
– This historic restaurant lies, surrounded by fishermen's cottages, directly on the Elbe and within sight of the Blue Miracle. It is sometimes somewhat loud, but very cosy; the Loschwitz artists often meet here for a drink of beer.

Weinbergschänke Pillnitz
Am Rathaus 2, 8054 Dresden.
Tel. 39805
– cosy restaurant near the Pillnitz Castle

Cafés

Café Pöppelmann in Hotel Bellevue
Köpckestr 15, 8060 Dresden
Tel. 53425
– Typically Saxon cakes are served and palm court music played in stylish surroundings.

Café Vis-á-vis in the Dresdner Hof
Brühlsche Terrasse, 8010 Dresden
Tel. 48410
– This fashionable café is in the Sekundo Genitur, the castle belonging to the second-born prince. During the summer months you can sit out on the Brühlsche Terrace, "The Balcony of Europe".

Confiserie Alte Münze
in the Dresdner Hof
Münzstr., 8010 Dresden
Tel. 48410

Café Prag
Altmarkt 16/17, 8010 Dresden
Tel. 4951135
– cosy mocha house with a view of the Altmarkt and the Church of the Cross

Wiener Café im Haus Altmarkt
Ernst-Thälmann-Str. 19-21,
8010 Dresden
Tel. 4951212

Café Kästner
Alaunstr. 1, 8060 Dresden
Tel. 570445
– The furnishing is orientated towards the literary figures' coffee houses of the 1920's; the café is dedicated to the author Erich Kästner, who was born in a house near-by.

Café Christian
Bautzner Str. 27 b, 8060 Dresden
Tel. 55751
– An exceptional feature are the alternating exhibitions, mostly of works by Dresden painters and graphic artists.

Café Toskana
Schillerplatz 1, 8053 Dresden
Tel. 30744
– The café is directly next to the Blue Miracle; it is famous for its excellent cakes.

Ice-cream Parlours

Eiscafé Kristall
Straße der Befreiung 2 a,
8060 Dresden
Tel. 55458

Eiscafé Schloßstraße
Schloßstraße 7, 8010 Dresden
Tel. 4951154

Eiscafé Barbarine
Prager Straße, 8010 Dresden
Tel. 436255

Der Eisgarten Huß
Alttolkewitz 31, 8021 Dresden
Tel. 32684
– pleasant family business with very good ice-cream

Eispavillon
Bärensteiner Str. 1, 8021 Dresden
Tel. 38619

Night Clubs

Café Prag
Altmarkt 16/17, 8010 Dresden
Tel. 4951135
– for decades, the only variety entertainment in the DDR

Club Alibi in the Dresdner Hof
An der Frauenkirche 5, 8010 Dresden
Tel. 48410

Mazurka Bar in the International
Prager Str., 8010 Dresden
Tel. 4952565

Tanzbar Baltic in the Hotel Newa
(bar with dancing)
Leningrader Str., 8010 Dresden
Tel. 4967112

Tanzbar Haus Altmarkt
(bar with dancing)
Ernst-Thälmann-Str. 19/21,
8010 Dresden,
Tel. 4951212

Tanzbar Parkhotel
(bar with dancing)
Bautzner Landstr. 7, 8051 Dresden
Tel. 36851

Tanzbar in the Luisenhof
(bar with dancing)
Bergbahnstr. 8, 8051 Dresden
Tel. 36842

Discotheques

Jugendcafé Festival
(Café for Young People)
Ernst-Thälmann-Str. 24,
8010 Dresden
Tel. 4951281

Herkuleskeule
Hans-Beimler-Platz, 8010 Dresden
Tel. 4955191

Jugendtanzgaststätte Parkhotel
(Young People's Dancing)
Bautzner Landstr. 7, 8051 Dresden
Tel. 36851

Lindengarten
Otto-Buchwitz-Str. 121 a,
8060 Dresden,
Tel. 55921

Café Heiderand
Siegfried-Rädel-Platz 4,
8052 Dresden
Tel. 36166

Casinos

CD Casino Dresden in Hotel Bellevue
Köpckestr. 15, 8060 Dresden
Tel. 53425
– roulette, black jack, slot-machines, open daily from 7 pm

Moulin Rouge
Gostritzer Straße 18, 8020 Dresden
– roulette and other games of chance

Pubs, with Accents on Particular Scenes

The Dresden scene is concentrated in the outlying districts of Neustadt, a run-down residential area built at the end of the 19th century - but it possesses a certain degenerate charm. Even before the "change" in 1989 an alternative culture had developed in occupied houses here - tolerated by the SED state with bad grace. It is hardly surprising that the social situation came to a head: only some of the houses can be renovated, and the property situation is still not clear. The town authorities declared the outlying districts of Neustadt to be a "protected area", which hardly helped at all. The young people reacted in their own way to the Reunification, which seemed ominous to them: in June 1990 they occupied the outlying districts of Neustadt and proclaimed the "Motley Republic of Neustadt".

And the activities here really are motley, in spite of the leaking roofs and crumbling facades. Very soon numerous pubs, cafés, galleries and theatres sprung up in the dilapidated houses. In the legal void immediately following the "change" nobody bothered about trade licences or closing time, and a most fascinating alternative culture developed – it is an absolutely unique one of its kind. The scene is characterized by creativity, not violence; and it looks as though, in spite of unsolved conflicts, the "Motley Republic of Neustadt" is flexible enough to keep going – even under the conditions of market economy.

Night life in Dresden, until recently non-existent, has been made possible here; things are lively and highly interesting into the early hours.

Café Stillos
Hechtstr. 26, 8060 Dresden
– meeting place for punks and dropouts

Stadt Riesa e.V.
Adlergasse 14, 8060 Dresden
– gallery, reading café, restaurant. There are plans for a graphic printer's, a health food store, vegetarian meals, a day-nursery and a playgroup.

Die Bronxx
Alaunstr. 64, 8060 Dresden
– artists' pub, gallery, frequent readings

Stettiner Hof Café Spitz
Friedrich-Wolf-Str. 18, 8060 Dresden
– live blues music

Galeriecafé "100"
Alaunstr. 100, 8060 Dresden
– here there is often jazz; as in many of the other pubs in Neustadt, you can also drink your red wine by candlelight in the ramschackle backyard gardens.

Tivoli
Louisenstr. 10, 8060 Dresden
– The "seat of government" of the Motley Republic, for this is where the "monarch without portfolio" holds court. The guests are entertained with accordion music – whether they like it or not.

Galeriecafé Planwirtschaft (Gallery Café Planned Economy)
Louisenstr. 20, 8060 Dresden
– The name is a reminder of former times, hardly mourned by the people who sit here until the break of day.

Cinemas

Filmtheater Prager Straße
Round cinema and studio theatre
Prager Straße 1, 8010 Dresden
Tel. 4952025

Filmtheater Schauburg
Otto-Buchwitz-Str. 55, 8060 Dresden
Tel. 570835

Filmtheater Faunpalast
Leipziger Str. 76, 8023 Dresden
Tel. 54550

Filmtheater Ost
Schandauer Str. 72, 8021 Dresden
Tel. 333782

Parklichtspiele Weißer Hirsch
Bautzner Landstr. 6, 8051 Dresden
Tel. 36585

Stephenson Lichtspiele
Stephensonstr. 40, 8045 Dresden
Tel. 2231403

Filmtheater Olympia
Dohnaer Str. 55, 8020 Dresden
Tel. 479717

Filmtheater Reick
Reicker Str. 39, 8036 Dresden
Tel. 472079

Filmtheater Gittersee
Karlsruher Str. 136, 8040 Dresden
Tel. 478347

Filmtheater Turmhaus Cotta
Grillparzer Str. 51,
8029 Dresden, Tel. 434304

Filmtheater am Hauptbahnhof
(Cinema at the Main Station)
Wiener Piatz, 8010 Dresden,
Tel. 470532

Celebrations and Festivals

Frühlingsfest – spring festival – (May), Vogelwiese (August), Herbstfest – autumn festival – (October)
– traditional fun-fairs with beer tents and carousels at the Fucikplatz

International Dixieland Festival
– during the first half of May

Dresden Music Festival
with the International Carl-Maria-von-Weber Competition
– international music and theatre festival at the end of May and beginning of June

Park Festival
– an open-air rock festival in August - its future is uncertain due to financial difficulties

International Hit Festival
– took place up to now in September

Strietzelmarkt
– Dresden Christmas Market with a centuries-old tradition – takes place on the Altmarkt

Observation Points

Town Hall Tower (Rathausturm)
– There is a lift up to the observation platform at a height of 86m; the Town Hall Tower is in all 98m high. The entrance is from the Kreuzstraße.

Luisenhof
Bergbahnstr. 8, 8051 Dresden
– The restaurant is called "Dresden's Balcony" because of the fantastic view from there of the town and the Elbe Valley. One way to reach the Luisenhof is by the Funicular Railway from the Körnerplatz.

Loschwitzhöhe
– At the top of the Cable Railway there is an observation terrace with a lovely view.

Television Tower (Fernsehturm)
Oberwachwitzer Weg 37,
8054 Dresden
– If the weather is right, you can see a long way from the observation platform or the café at a height of 148 m of the 252 m high Television Tower - into "Saxon Switzerland", the East Ore Mountains, the Lausitz Hills and over to Meissen.

Fichteturm
Fichtepark Westenedring, 8060 Dresden
– The 25 m high tower was opened in 1896; it is Dresden's oldest observation tower.

Walks

Route 1: From the Main Station to the Cathedral

To the north, the Main Station is followed by the Wiener Platz and the Prager Straße, built around the turn of the century. In the 1920's, the Prager Straße, as a promenade, could compete with the Kurfürstendamm in Berlin or the Maximilianstraße in Munich.

Nowadays it is a pedestrian precinct, lined with partly monotonous, partly monstrous buildings of the 1970's. In October 1989 violent demonstrations took place here in connection with the journey through Dresden of the refugees from the German Embassy in Prague; they were one of the reasons for the overthrow of the SED (Communist Party) and the reunification of Germany. Past fountains, green areas, hotels, shops and restaurants, a cinema and a department store you reach, via the Waisenhausstraße and the Dr. Külz-Ring, the Altmarkt (Old Market). On the right hand side you can see the New Town Hall with its 98 m high tower, topped by the gilded figure of Hercules.

On the east side of the Altmarkt is the Kreuzkirche (Church of the Cross); the west side was built in Stalinist neo-baroque in the 1950's. On the ground floor there are shops and restaurants (Café Prag). East of the Altmarkt, beyond the busy Ernst-Thälmann-Straße, stands the bulky edifice of the Palace of Culture (1968), in which there are a concert hall, a theatre and a restaurant. We pass it on the right hand side and arrive, via the Galleriestraße, at the Neumarkt (New Market), which is dominated by the impressive ruins of the Frauenkirche (Church of Our Lady). It is next door to the hotel Dresdner Hof, which was opened in 1990. To the left you can see the burned-out ruins of the Castle, being rebuilt, and in front of it, the Johanneum, now housing the Transport Museum.

To the right, next to the Johanneum and through an archway, you enter the Stallhof (Stable Court), its impressive renaissance architecture overwhelming. The bronze columns of the "ringshooting course", the only remaining one in Europe, date back to 1601 (G.M. Nosseni and B. Bachstädt). Also preserved are the bath and the trough for the horses that were originally kept in the Johanneum. Instead of races, concerts take place here now. The Augustusstraße is closed in to the right by the Landtag (State Parliament), which was built by the architect of the Berlin Reichstag, Paul Wallot (1901-03). On the left hand side, on the outer side of the Langer Gang (Long Passage) is the Fürstenzug (Parade of Princes), 102 m long, a series of paintings. The view through the Augustusstraße to the Catholic Hofkirche (Court Church) is the only remaining architectural vista in Dresden to present itself as it was before the destruction. The Langer Gang is followed by the Georgentor (George Gate), built in neo-renaissance style, and until 1918 the residence of the Saxon kings. You can enter the Hofkirche by the side door. A tour of the church is highly recommended.

Route 2: From the Albertinum to the Zwinger

Presented in the Albertinum are the most important museums of the Staatliche Kunstsammlungen (State Art Collections), including the Grünes Gewölbe (Green Vault), the Paintings Gallery, the Sculpture Collection and the Münzkabinett (Collection of Coins and Medals). It forms the east end of the Brühlsche Terrasse. In the park there are monuments to Caspar David Friedrich and the alchemist Johann Friedrich Böttger, who invented the European hard porcelain, Meissen porcelain, in the casemates of the Brühlsche Terrasse. One part of the casemates has been turned into the popular student club "Bärenzwinger" (Bear Pit), the entrance of which is visible from above. The Delphinbrunnen (Delphin Fountain), surrounded by a wrought-iron railing, is a baroque construction by the

Georg-Treu-Platz

Frenchman Pierre Coudray (mid-18th century) and is the last reminder of the time when the terrace was part of the private garden of Count Brühl. To the west of the Albertinum a twin staircase leads to the Georg-Treu-Platz, where there is also an entrance to the Green Vault. The statue of Gottfried Semper stands at the top of the stairs. The next buildings on the Brühlsche Terrasse were constructed in 1891-94 by Konstantin Lipsius for the Saxon Kunstverein (Art Society) and the Dresden Academy of Art. From the railing of the Brühlsche Terrasse, looking up the Elbe to the east, you have a fantastic view of the delightful Elbe countryside. Unfortunately the view is spoiled by two bulky new buildings. On the other bank of the Elbe, beyond a modern bridge (a replacement for the Carola Bridge, which was destroyed during the war), is the Gesamtministerium (General Ministry – 1904-06) and, directly opposite, the former Finanzministerium (Ministry of Finance (1889-94).

The Secundo Genitur was built on the site of Count Brühl's library in 1897, a small neo-baroque palace which was intended for the second-born prince. After being rebuilt it was used as a restaurant. Today it is part of the Hotel Dresdener Hof, with which it is connected by a covered bridge. During the summer you can sit outside the "Café Vis-á-vis" and enjoy the view from the Brühlsche Terrasse. Directly in front of it stands the monument to Dresden's most important sculptor, Ernst Rietschel. At the end of the Brühlsche Terrasse is the Ständehaus (building with the "Realms of the State", 1901-03), built for the Saxon Landtag (State Parliament). At present the only partly reerected house contains the Saxon Landesamt für Denkmalpflege (State Office for the Conservation of Monuments), the Museum of Mineralogy and Geology, the Museum für Tierkunde (Museum of Zoology) and the German Fotothek. The Brühlsche Terrasse was opened to the public in 1814 by the Russian military commandant, Prince Repnin. This terrace, known as the "Balcony of Europe" entices you to stroll. At the west end of the Terrace is the magnificent flight of steps designed by Gottlob Friedrich Thormayer, flanked by the groups of figures depicting the four seasons (sculptor Johannes Schilling). From the Castle Square, past the Catholic Court Church, you come to the Theaterplatz, one of the most beautiful squares in Germany. On a high pedestal in the centre of the square stands the equestrian statue of the artistic King Johann. The west side of the square is dominated by the Semper Opera. On the side facing the Elbe is the building "Italienisches Dörfchen" (Italian Village), at present a closed restaurant. It's name is a reminder that the Italian craftsmen who built the Court Church in the 18th century lived on this very spot. Gottfried Semper's gallery building on the opposite side of the square forms the end of the Zwinger facing the Elbe. On the right side of the

Zwinger, Inner Court

Sophienstraße is the classical building of the Altstädter Wache (Guard-House), the only work by Schinkel in Dresden; nowadays it is used as the theatre advance booking office. To the left the ruined building of the Castle – you can see that work has been started on it. The Carillon Pavilion leads on to the spacious inner courtyard of the Zwinger.

Route 3: From the Castle Square to the Japanese Palace

When Napoleon marched into Dresden in 1812 a triumphal arch was erected for him. The square on which the emperor stood was marked with an N, which is still visible. We step onto the Augustusbrücke (Augustus Bridge), which is the oldest bridge in the Dresden town area. As early as 1275 there were references made to a bridge at this point. Enlarged and altered in 1727-31 by the master architect of the Zwinger, Matthäus Daniel Pöppelmann, it was regarded as one of the most beautiful in Germany. However, its 25 arches became a hinderance to the developing shipping and in 1907 had to give way to the present bridge, which was blown up in 1945 by an SS commando troop and rebuilt by 1949. Looking back from the middle of the bridge, you have a good view of the picturesque moorings of the White Fleet at the Terrassenufer and of the Brühlsche Terrasse. To the left, on the Altstadt side, you can see the Semper Opera, the huge reservoirs on the bank of the Elbe and behind the Marienbrücke the glass dome of the cigarette factory Yenidze, built in the shape of a mosque in 1907. At the Neustadt end of the bridge, to the left, is the so-called Blockhaus ("Log Cabin"), a baroque edifice, which in the past served as the seat of the Saxon Ministry of War. The next buildings are the Hotel Bellevue and the Japanese Palace.

On the Neustadt side, you use the pedestrian subway to reach the Neustadt Market, where the equestrian statue of August the Strong stands. After the city fire of 1685,

Equestrian Statue of August the Strong

which destroyed the whole of the Neustadt of today, originally called Altendresden, the whole district was rebuilt by August the Strong to a well-balanced plan. The present street layout dates from that time. Apart from that, unfortunately, only little of the historic Neustadt remains. In 1979 the reconstruction of the former Hauptstraße, which had been renamed "Liberation Street" in 1945, was completed. Instead of the magnificent baroque houses the street is now lined with dreary new buildings. That some of its flair could still be retained is due to the large plain trees and the tastefully arranged gardens in the centre of the wide avenue. At the lower end, on the left hand side of the street, some of the baroque houses were spared the air-raid, one of them being the famous Kügelgenhaus. They were restored and now convey an impression of the former glory of this street. The painter Wilhelm von Kügelgen, in his famous work "Recollections of an Old Man", describes it as "Dresden's most beautiful and lively street". Thanks to the many shops (incl. 3 bookshops and an antique shop), restaurants and cafés it is still alive today.

The Dreikönigskirche (Epiphany Church), the left front of which borders the street and is crowned by a magnificent tympanum, is at present the seat of the Saxon State Parliament. We pass the Schiller Memorial, turn left at the "Platz der Einheit" (Unity Square) and go through the Friedrich-Engels-Straße back towards the Elbe. This street, in which the magnificent baroque houses have only been partly restored, leads into the Karl-Marx-Platz, with its large cascading fountain. Behind it the outlines of the Japanese Palace come into sight. To the right is the memorial to Friedrich August der Gerechte (Friedrich August the Just). We pass this and enter a spacious park, which adjoins the gardens of the Hotel Bellevue. From here you have the famous view of the Altstadt. It was made familiar to anyone interested in art by the Canaletto painting – to be seen here in the gallery.

Route 4: Along the Altstadt bank of the Elbe to the Blue Miracle

This tour is only for those who have time and are used to walking. However, this 5 km stretch is well worth the effort. Nowhere else can you experience the harmony of landscape and architecture which is so characteristic of Dresden as on the old towpath, on which the "Bomätscher", as the people who towed were called in Saxony, pulled their boats upstream before steamships were introduced. Our walk begins on the Terrassenufer where the paddle-steamers and motorboats of the White Fleet are moored.

First we walk upstream, then under the new bridge to the next crossing. To the left the Brücke der Einheit (Unity Bridge) – the former Albertbrücke – stretches across the river. To the right is the impressive Amtsgericht (County Court), built by A. Roßbach (1890-92). From there we go directly down to the Elbwiesen (Elbe meadows). The Elbe flows in a light curve to the right. We can see the Rose Garden on the opposite bank, a small well-kept park. The meadows grow wider and often one can find here, in the middle of a city with half a million inhabitants, a peacefully grazing flock of sheep. Soon the building complex of the Diakonissenhaus on the Neustadt side becomes visible. The two parts of the city are connected here by a small ferry. Next to the Diakonissenhaus is the Drachenschänke, an historic inn. The Linkesche Bad, a popular tourist inn with theatre performances stood somewhere here. It went down in literature through E.T.A. Hoffmann's fairy tale "The Golden Pot". Just a little further on we can see the "Waldschlößchen" brewery.

Far less pleasing are the bulky buildings which served the Stasi (DDR State Security) right up until the autumn of 1989. Now they are used by medical institutes. Not far from here there begins the most pleasant part of the Elbe banks in Dresden. The three Elbe castles, Albrechtsberg Castle, Villa Stockhausen and Eckberg Castle stand on what used to be vineyards. Somewhat hidden is the summer house of August the Strong's court jeweller, Johann Melchior Dinglinger. Round the bend in the river the Blue Miracle comes into view; with its double-arch, filigree iron construction it spans the Elbe and connects the former villages of Blasewitz and Loschwitz.

The Loschwitz slopes, the upper part of which belongs to the former spa Weißer Hirsch, are studded with splendid 19th and 20th century villas. Also on the Loschwitz bank of the Elbe is the house of the Körner family, with whom Schiller spent a great deal of time. The Schillerplatz with its historic restaurant "Schiller Garden", named after its prominent guest, is an architecturally impressive late 19th century shopping centre. From here you can take a taxi or tram back to the city centre.

Route 5: From the Schillerplatz up to the Weißer Hirsch

You walk over the Blue Miracle to the former wine and fishing village Loschwitz, which has, due to its pleasant surroundings, been a favourite

Brühlsche Terrace Steps

castle. Although untrue, the story of a Dresden industrialist is still told, who on the night of February 13th 1945 stood on this hill and guided the English bombers in. The restaurant Luisenhof, known as "Dresden's Balcony" is highly recommended for, among other things, its fantastic view. In good weather the terrace is ideal. Weißer Hirsch had its heyday as a world-famous spa at the beginning of this century. Hardly anywhere else in Europe has a residential area of the industrial and Art Nouveau periods been so well preserved as here. During the war the Lahmann Sanatorium was closed. Later, the Soviet Army took it over and used it as a hospital, to the detriment of the Spa park – its former beauty can only be imagined. However, after the departure of the Soviet Army there will be a renaissance of the Weißer Hirsch as a spa. The research institute of the famous Manfred von Ardenne has been here in Weißer Hirsch for the last 40 years. In a way his famous therapies (including those for cancer, heart and circulatory complaints) keep on the tradition of the Lahmann Sanatorim. On leaving the Bergbahnstraße you go through the Plattleite to reach the Bautzner Landstraße. The former sanatorium, the spa house and the once fashionable Park Hotel make up the centre of the village.

On the other side of the Bautzner Landstraße is the Dresden Heide with its Waldpark, tennis courts and concert stand. The two mineral springs (Degele and Schwestern) in the Stechgrund provide water that does not only taste good but is good for one's health as well. From the Park Hotel you can return to the town centre by taxi or tram.

Weißer Hirsch, Villa Elbblick

Excursions

National Park Sächsische Schweiz (Saxon Switzerland)

The romantic and picturesque Elbe Sandstone Mountains were made popular towards the end of the 18th century by the Swiss painter Anton Graff and his countryman, the copper engraver Adrian Zingg. These two gave "Saxon Switzerland" its name, although there is hardly any similarity with the alpine republic. This small mountain range with its steep faces and rocky peaks is a playground for mountaineers and its table mountains remind one rather of the Sierra Nevada. The highest points of this 368 sq km large national park are the Zschirnstein (560 m above sea-level), the Pfaffenstein (429 m above sea-level) and the Lilienstein (412 m above sea-level). The most comfortable and at the same time interesting way to get to know Saxon Switzerland is by taking a trip with one of the nostalgic paddle-steamers of the White Fleet. From April until October the boats leave several times a day from their moorings at the Terrassenufer, travelling upstream to Bad Schandau or Schmilka.

After leaving the city, past Loschwitz and Blasewitz, the boat soon reaches Pillnitz, with the impressive view of the castle facing the water. After passing through the not particularly pleasant industrial town of Heidenau you come to the medieval town of Pirna, which is also known as the "Gate to Saxon Switzerland". Pirna's medieval town centre is certainly worth visiting; it has been essentially preserved as is shown on one of Canaletto's famous topographic town views. With the Marienkirche (St. Mary's Church) from the first half of the 16th century, Pirna has one of the most beautiful and valuable Gothic churches in Saxony. Sonnenstein Castle crowns the town.

The villages Zeichen, Wehlen and Rathen lie at the foot of the ever steeper towering sandstone hills. Those who wish to climb up to the Bastei (Bastion), one of Europe's most beautiful vantage points, have to leave the boat at Rathen. From the steep rock ridge, on which there is an hotel and a large restaurant with a terrace, you have a magnificent view of the mountains and the labyrinthine gorges. (En route by car, see Stolpen.) In Rathen there is a Felsenbühne (natural mountain stage) on which, in the summer months, popular plays (Karl May a.o.) are performed. After Rathen the Elbe winds its way round a narrow bend; to the left is Lilienstein, to the right the fortress Königstein. The boats stop off at the small town of the same name at the foot of the fortress. What Spandau was for Prussia, Königstein was for Saxony: state prison, and refuge for the royal court in uncertain times. Many a legend has grown up around the Königstein, first mentioned in 1241 and converted into the famous fortress at the beginning of the 18th century. Peter the Great and Napoleon came to visit the fortress. One of the inmates of Königstein was the Russian anarchist Michael Bakunin, as well as the social democrat August Bebel.

Johann Friedrich Böttger, the inventor of European hard porcelain, was a prisoner here in 1706 and 1707 and there is a memorial to him in the respective rooms. The many things worth seeing in the fortress include historic cannons, such as the "Faule Magd" (Lazy Maid) from the year 1450. The next stop is Bad Schandau, the most popular holiday resort and spa in Saxon Switzerland. The town church St. Johannes (17th and 18th centuries) is certainly worth a visit. The valuable renaissance altar (1575-79 by Hans Walther) was originally in the Church of the Cross in Dresden. The district Ostrau with its attractive half-timbered houses and small zoo can be reached by a 50 m high lift, which is considered to be a technical monument.

Bad Schandau is an ideal starting point for hikes in Saxon Switzerland. The Schrammsteine, about 3 km to the east, are easy to reach. The 4 km long, deeply fissured rock massif is one of the most beautiful of the whole mountain range. From the narrow trail you have a fantastic view of the whole area, including the Elbe canyon. Those who want to travel more comfortably can take the tram-like vehicle through the romantic Kirnitzsch Valley as far as the Lichtenhain waterfall.

Stolpen – Hohnstein – Bastei (Bastion)

Leave Dresden on the main road 6 in the direction of Bischofswerda. About 8 km past Weißig you turn right at the level of the village Fischbach and reach, after another 5 km, the small town of Stolpen.

The castle stands on a basalt hilltop south of the town - it probably dates back to the 12th century. In the 13th century the bishops of Meissen enlarged the fortresses on the border to Bohemia: the fortified towers, the cornhouse and the bishop's palace were built. In 1559 the castle came into the possession of the Saxon Elector. Stolpen became known through the famous Countess Cosel, August the Strong's mistress. After a dispute the king exiled her to Stolpen, where she remained from 1716 until her death in 1765. Her chambers in the so-called Cosel Tower have been preserved and are, together with other buildings, open to the public; the castle was partly destroyed by Napoleon in 1813. From Stolpen you drive on to Dobra, turn left there to Stürza, then via Heeselicht on to the picturesque small town of Hohnstein. The fortress Hohnstein, for a long time considered unconquerable, was a feared robber barons' hide-out during the Middle Ages. It did not come into the possession of the Wettins until 1443. August the Strong used it as a hunting lodge. Later it became a state prison. During the years 1933 and 1934 the Nazis used the castle as a concentration camp. Since 1951 it has been a youth hostel. In Hohnstein itself the baroque Stadtkirche (Town Church) is worth a visit. It was built in 1725-26 by the famous architect George Bähr. You leave Hohnstein in the direction of Lohmen; after about 3km you turn left and soon reach the Bastei. (See Excursion Saxon Switzerland)

Bautzen

Old Water Tower and Michaeli Church

You get to the town, which is about 50 km away from Dresden, on the main road 6 via Bischofswerda. At first you are surprised by a town silhouette which could hardly be more picturesque. High above the east bank of the Spree the towers of the more than 1000-year-old Ortenburg, the Michaeli Church and the Alte Wasserkunst (Old Waterworks) form an impressive ensemble.

The old Slavic settlement, first documented in 1002, owes its importance to the fact that it lay on the crossroads of two trading routes. After the settlement, Ortenburg was built as a border fortress by the Margrave of Meissen. Since 1635 the originally Bohemian town of Bautzen has belonged to Saxony. Unlike in Protestant Saxony, a large part of the population remained Catholic, as for a long time there was a Sorbic majority.

If you want to get to know Bautzen, you should do it on foot – from the leaning Reichen Tower to the pedestrian precinct in the Reichenstraße. On this most important main street there are magnificent and well-restored houses of the renaissance, baroque and rococo periods. To the west is the Hauptmarkt (Main Market). The Cathedral of St. Peter is interesting – its oldest parts date back to the second half of the 13th century. It is divided fairly between Protestants and Catholics, the two halves being separated by a wrought-iron trellis in the middle. Behind it is the cathedral chapter, with its magnificent portal facing the street. If you are lucky you will be admitted to the cathedral treasure chamber which has a remarkable collection of sacred works of art. It is better to make an appointment by telephone first (Bautzen 44102). Through narrow alleyways you can walk to the Catholic Nikolai Cemetery, dating back to 1455. The graves are grouped around a ruined Gothic church and the atmosphere of this little churchyard is reminiscent of paintings by Caspar David Friedrich. A little further on you get to the Ortenburg, only part of which is open to the public. For those interested in the history of the Sorbs, the only national minority in the former DDR, information can be obtained from the Museum for the History and Culture of the Sorbs (Ortenburg 5, Tel. 42294. Open daily 9.30 a.m.-12.30 p.m. and 1.30 p.m.-4.00 p.m. Closed on the first Monday in the month). The tower of the Old Waterworks offers a good overall view of the almost 1000-year-old town and its surroundings.

Right next to the Reichen Tower is the Stadtmuseum (Town Museum): it was founded in 1868 and has a very good collection. (Tel. Bautzen 42064)

Großsedlitz Baroque Garden, Weesenstein and Kuckucksstein

On the main road 172 to Heidenau there is on the right hand side a signpost to the Großsedlitz Baroque Garden, which is only a few kilometres further on. It is the most perfect French-style baroque park in Saxony. After August the Strong had purchashed this property from Graf Wackerbarth in 1723, the most prominent architects in Dresden were busy here until 1726. In this romantic park you can find works by nearly all of Dresden's eminent sculptors who had contributed to the Zwinger. The plans for the building of the castle were never carried out. From the Baroque Garden a little road leads into the Müglitztal (Müglitz Valley).

Weesenstein Castle is situated on a rock ledge high above the valley. It was built in the 14th century as a fortress, and converted and enlarged in the 16th and 17th centuries. The Weesenstein Castle Art Museum is well-known especially for its collection of historic wallpapers, which is well presented: the wallpapers are shown together with pieces of furniture of the respective periods. So you get some idea of the living conditions of past centuries. The chapel is also worth a visit. (8301 Weesenstein, Am Schloßberg 1, Tel. 238. Guided tours: March till November, Mon., Tues., Fri, 9 a.m., 11 a.m., 1.30 p.m., 3 p.m.; Sat. and Sun. 9 a.m., 11 a.m., 1 p.m., 2.30 p.m., 4 p.m.)

If you drive a few kilometres through the Müglitz Valley in the direction of Glashütte you soon reach Liebstadt. Kuckuckstein Castle is situated like a fairy-tale castle on a gneiss rock overlooking the dreamy little town. The castle was integrated into a 10th century fortress and last altered at the turn of the century. Of particular interest are the hunting, court and Napoleon rooms in the west wing, as well as the mighty keep.

The Freimaurerloge (Masonic Lodge) is something exceptional – the only one existing on the territory of the former DDR. (Kuckucksstein Castle Museum, Am Schloßberg 1, 8301 Liebstadt, Tel. 283. Guided tours Wed.-Fri. 10 a.m. and 2 p.m., Sat., Sun. and Hol. 10 a.m., 11 a.m, 2 p.m. and 3 p.m.)

Radebeul and Moritzburg

The Leipziger Straße leads to Radebeul, a town adjoining Dresden, between the Lößnitz vineyards and the banks of the Elbe. Travelling to Radebeul is like taking a journey back into childhood days, for this is the home of Winnetou and Old Shatterhand, Sam Hawkins and Kara Ben Nemsi. In Radebeul the Saxon author Karl May, who lived in the pompous Villa Shatterhand from 1896 until his death on March 30th 1912, thought up the fantastic stories that have fascinated generations. The villa now houses the Karl May Museum (Karl May Straße 5, 8122 Radebeul, Tel.

Dresden 73169. Open Tues. and Sun. 9a.m.-5p.m.). Some of Karl May's possessions are exhibited: oriental furniture, vessels and weapons. Three famous weapons are held as relīquia – "Henrystutzen", "Silberbüchse" and "Bärentöter". A well-arranged exhibition gives further information on the life and work of this controversial author. The Wild West itself begins out in the garden.

The Villa Bärenfett stands there – a large log cabin stuffed full with Indian objects of worship, chiefs' robes, weapons, jewellry and household articles: a unique European collection on the life of the North American prairie Indians.

Radebeul, Spitzhaus Restaurant

Another very interesting museum is in the Hoflößnitz Castle. This half-timbered building was erected from 1649 to 1650 as a summer residence for the Saxon Elector Johann Georg I; it is tucked away at the foot of the Radebeul vineyards. Particularly interesting is the hall on the first floor with its murals "Brasilian Birds". At the moment an exhibition is being prepared on the development of wine-growing in the Elbe Valley. (Museum Haus Hoflößnitz, Knohlweg 37, 8122 Radebeul, Tel. Dresden 75616. Open April till November, Wed. 2 p.m.-6 p.m., Thurs. and Fri. 2-4 p.m., Sat.10 a.m.-4 p.m. and Sun. 2-5 p.m.)

You should leave your car in Radebeul (Weißes Roß) and take the historic narrow-gauge railway train through the vineyards to Moritzburg. Moritzburg lies in an idyllic area with small lakes, which at one time was one of the favourite hunting grounds of the Saxon Electors. The most important thing to look at here is the impressive baroque castle.

(Baroque Museum, Moritzburg Castle, 8105 Moritzburg, Tel. 439. Open March till October, Tues.-Sun. 9 a.m.-12 a.m. and 1 p.m.-4.45 p.m., November and February Wed.-Sun. 9 a.m.-12 a.m. and 1 p.m.-3.45 p.m. Guided tours every 60 minutes.)

The four-wing complex with four round turrets and a chapel in the west wing stands on an island in the

Moritzburg Castle

middle of the Large Lake. Originally only a rather simple hunting lodge stood here, built by Duke Moritz in the 16th century and named after him. August the Strong, however, had it altered into a splendid hunting lodge by the builder of the Zwinger, Pöppelmann, and the two Frenchmen Zacharia Longuelune and Jean de Bodt in 1723-27. Moritzburg played an important role in the Augustian ceremonies. Not only the castle, but the whole of the surrounding area was used for these grand festivities. On the Large Lake to the east August had a lighthouse and a harbour built for himself as a back-

Harbour with lighthouse

ground for the naval battles he enacted. Not far from the lighthouse is the Fasanenschlößchen ("Little Pheasants Castle"), a small rococo building dating back to 1770-82; it now houses an ornithological exhibition put on by the Dresden Zoological Museum. (Tel. 207. Open from March 15th to October 31st daily 9 a.m.-4 p.m.)

The former Electoral "Waldschenke", not far from the Fasanenschlößchen, was built in 1770. Today it is a well-known historic restaurant with partly original furnishings, a large garden for guests and several hotel rooms. (Waldschenke, 8105 Moritzburg. Tel. 489).

Hardly less popular is Adams Gasthof (Tel. 431), an inn with a long tradition. The small but unusually good wine restaurant "Das Kneipchen" was opened only recently (Ernst-Thälmann-Allee 37, 8105 Moritzburg. Tel 242). The charming landlady succeeds in proving that Saxon cooking is far better than its reputation.

Meissen

To be reached on the main road 6 (or by the S-Bahn train in 35 minutes).

After passing Scharfenberg, the pretty Spar Hills with their terraced vineyards come into sight on the opposite side of the Elbe. Shortly afterwards you have a view of the famous silhouette of the town, the high-lying Albrechtsburg Castle and the filigree double-towered front of the medieval cathedral. It is advisable to leave your car on one of the parking lots on the bank of the Elbe. You can only get to know this medieval town with its winding alleys (and numerous one-way streets) on foot. In 929 Heinrich I founded the castle "Misni" in order to subjugate the Slavic native population. The diocese originated in 968, the town itself was first mentioned in 1225. But Meissen is more than simply a small Saxon town. For centuries the bishops and margraves of Meissen had great political influence.

Not until 1485 did the Wettins transfer their residence from Meissen to Dresden. Thus Meissen lost its political power, but in 1710 the Royal Porcelain Manufactory was founded in the Albrechtsburg in Meissen, which later made the town world-famous.

The most suitable place to start on your tour of the town is the Markt. On the north side is the Rathaus (Town Hall), built by Arnold von Westphalen in 1472, the striking thing about it being the three late-Gothic decoration gables.

The Marktapotheke (Chemist's), Markt 4, built in the middle of the 16th century, is one of the most beautiful houses in the town. It is worth looking at the richly decorated interior of the Gothic Frauenkirche (Church of Our Lady); in 1929 the first porcelain carillon in the world was installed in its tower – it can be heard on the hour. The well-known wine restaurant Vincenz Richter (Tel. 3285) has existed in the half-timbered house Am Markt 12 since 1873; it is furnished with historic weapons, armour and instruments of torture. Over the steps Superintendentenstufen and the Freiheit you come to the former monastery St. Afra. It was here that the first parish church of the town was built in the 11th century. At the beginning of the 13th century it had to give way to the new building of the Augustiner-Chorherrnstift (Augustiner Men's Choir Foundation). Worth seeing are the early baroque carved altar (about 1660) and the wooden pulpit (1657). As a consequence of the Reformation the monastery was secularized in 1540. In its rooms Elector Moritz established the first Saxon "royal school", an elite school, whose pupils were chosen on the grounds of their abilities, regardless of their social standing. Among the best-known former pupils are the poets Lessing and Gellert, the satirist Gottlob Wilhelm Rabener and the founder of homoeopathy, Samuel Hahnemann.

A plaque on the Burglehen Freiheit 2 is a reminder that the painter Ludwig Richter lived here from 1828 to 1836. Across the castle bridge and through the portal, which is decorated with two mosaic pictures (by the creator of the "Parade of Princes" mural, Wilhelm Walther), you come to the Burgberg (castle hill).

The cathedral, which is considered to be one of the most important Gothic buildings in Germany, was built on the site of a former Romanesque edifice between the years 1260 and 1410. The west towers,which had been started on at the beginning of the 14th century, were destroyed by a storm in 1413. Reconstructed in the 15th century, they were again destroyed by lightning in 1547. The present towers, which appear so convincingly Gothic in design, were not erected until 1903-1908 by the winner of an architectural competition, Karl Schäfer from Karlsruhe. Worthy of mention are, among the valuable, mainly medieval furnishings, the statues of the patrons and founders of the High Choir. The figures are made of sandstone and have coloured settings; they are probably the work of the "Naumburg Master" and are among the best 13th century sculptures in Central Europe. The lay altar in front of the choir screen is from the studio of Lucas Cranach the Elder, the tombs in the Electoral funeral chapel partly from Vischer's studio in Nuremberg. In the cathedral, which became Protestant during the Reformation, there are frequently organ and choral concerts.

The Albrechtsburg, built at the turn of the 15th to the 16th century to plans by Arnold von Westphalen, is an example of the transition from the medieval castle,with its function to defend and protect, to the castle as a symbol of royal prestige. The Albrechtsburg is the most important German secular building put up towards the end of the Middle Ages. Special mention must be made of the masterful court facade with the Large Wendelstein, an unprecedented architectural achievement. The vaults of the inner rooms are also famous – the light and shadow effects make the architecture appear to almost come alive.

Planned originally as a residence for the Wettins, the castle could never fulfill this function, for due to the division of the country in 1485 the Albertine residence was moved to Dresden. The castle didn't gain importance until 1710 when August the Strong founded the first European porcelain manufactory here. After the manufactory was moved to the Triebisch Valley in 1863, the castle was renovated and decorated with a great series of murals depicting the history of the House of Wettin; the work was done by Dresden painters of historical sce-

Moritzburg Castle

Moritzburg, Fasanenschlößchen

nes. Today Albrechtsburg is both an architectural monument and a museum (Domplatz 1, 8025 Meissen, Tel. 2920). It contains an exhibition on the history of building, as well as an interesting collection of sacred sulptures from the 12th to the 16th centuries. Chamber concerts are held frequently in the banquet hall. From the terrace between the cathedral and the Bishop's Palace you have a fantastic view of the bizarre pattern of roofs of the medieval town – and the Elbe Valley. The State Porcelain Manufactory (Leninplatz 9, 8250 Meissen, Tel. 541. Open April-October, Tues.-Sun. 8 a.m.-4 p.m.) exhibits a collection of about 3500 pieces of all periods. It is also interesting to visit the workshops (open 8 a.m.-12 a.m. and 1 p.m-3 p.m.) where you can watch the modellers and hand-painters at work and follow the individual phases of completion.
Whilst in Meissen you shouldn't under any circumstances miss tasting the good-quality Meissen wine. Less

Meissen, Vincenz Richter

well-known, but just as recommendable as the Vincenz Richter restaurant which is perpetually besieged by tourists, is the "Bauernhäusel", a restaurant on the other side of the Elbe – a little way up the river, at the foot of the gentle Spar Hills. (Obersparer Str. 20, 8025 Meissen, Tel 3317)

If you want to see something of the wine district, you should drive down the Elbe on the Neustadt (new town) side as far as Diesbar-Seußlitz, the prettiest of all the wine villages on the Elbe. Standing on the slope above the village is the little Baroque Castle, built by George Bähr in 1725, with its adjoining park. At the inn "Zum Roß" you can sit on the terrace near the river and enjoy a glass of wine, together with a tasty and unbelievably cheap meal. (8401 Seußlitz, Elbstr. 25). It is surprising how many pleasant wine taverns there are, especially along the Elbstraße, when you think of how gastronomy in the former DDR was neglected. Particularly to be recommended is the "Seußlitzer Weinstuben" (8401 Seußlitz, Elbstraße 26, Tel. 236), a tasteful, historic restaurant with a shady garden and several simply-furnished hotel rooms.

Freiberg

Take the main road 173 (or a train from the Main Station). In 1168 silver was found in the Ore-Mountains. By amalgamating four mining villages, the town of Freiberg was soon founded; as a mining centre, it was largely responsible for Saxony's wealth. The economic importance of the town even led to its becoming Germany's first "free mining town".

The Mining Academy was founded in 1765 and still exists today; students there included Alexander von Humboldt, Novalis, Theodor Körner and the Russian scientist Lomonossow.

The economic power is reflected by the extravagance of the architecture of the town. The most prominent building is the Cathedral, built on the site of a former Romanesque edifice around the turn of the 15th to the 16th century. The Freiberg cathedral is the first Upper Saxon hall church of the Late Gothic period. From 1541 to 1694 the Wettins used the chancel as a place of burial. For this purpose the Late Gothic chancel was changed between 1585 and 1649 into a mixture of renaissance and baroque styles – to plans by the Italian Giovanni Maria Nosseni. The sculptured decoration of the ceiling with "The Second Coming" is an exceptional work of art. Hardly any other German pulpits are as beautiful in their filigree work as the "Tulip Pulpit", created by Hans Witten in 1508-10. The "Golden Portal" is also very impressive – it is a Late Romanesque framed portal, rich with sculptural ornimentation. The large Organ, which is known for the purity and beauty of its tone, was built in 1711-14 by the famous Gottfried Silbermann, who also built the smaller organ on the east gallery. The royal gallery – to mention only one of the cathedral's invaluable furnishings – was put up in 1726-27 to designs by the builder of the Zwinger, Pöppelmann.

Freiberg has two further Gothic churches, the Nikolai Church and the Petri Church; part of their mostly baroque furnishings remain. Both the Nikolai Church and the New-Gothic Jacobi Church possess an organ made by Gottfried Silbermann.

The Town Hall (Rathaus) on the east side of the Obermarkt was built at the beginning of the 15th century. The town's Coat of Arms (1510) can be seen over the baroque main portal. The tower was reerected in 1471 after a fire and raised in 1618.

The Town and Mining Museum (Am Dom 1, 9200 Freiberg, Tel. 3197) is located in the Domherrenhaus (1484), one of the most beautiful buildings in the old part of the town. The exhibition illustrates the development of mining in Freiberg and its connection with the history of the town. A collection of sacred wooden figures by Freiberg artists is particularly interesting.

The Instruction Mine "Alte Elisabeth" of the Freiberg Mining Academy (Fuchsmühlenweg, 9200 Freiberg, Tel. 2044) was set up in a closed-down mine. You have to book if you want to visit the underground area. The installations above ground (Open from May till October, Sat. 8 a.m.-11 a.m.) are in a building complex which has remained almost unchanged since the 15th century, including all the necessary rooms and silver-mining equipment.

Toy Town Seiffen

To be reached on the main road 170, exit Obercarsdorf via Frauenstein, Rechenberg-Bienenmühle and Neuhausen. Seiffen is situated in the East Ore-Mountains, to the south of the Schwartenberg (789 m above sea level); it is not only a popular spa, but also the centre of the famous Ore-Mountains toy industry. Both children and collectors love the animal loops, the carved figures holding candles, the fumigating figures, the nutcrackers and Christmas pyramids, which have been produced by homeworkers for centuries.

Of course the most important thing to see is the Ore-Mountains Toy Museum (Ernst-Thälmann-Str. 73, 9335 Seiffen, Tel. 239. Open daily 9 a.m.-12 a.m. and 1 p.m.-5 p.m.). The comprehensive collection does not only include the most beautiful toys and Christmas decorations, but it also shows you, in a true to the original toymaker's workshop, how these little marvels of craftsmanship are made.

In the Open-Air Museum (Freilichtmuseum, Ernst-Thälmann-Str. 203, 9335 Seiffen, Tel. 388. Open April-October, Sat. - Thurs. 9 a.m. - 12 a.m., 1 p.m.-5 p.m.), with its historic buildings and original tools, you can learn about handicraft and living conditions in the Middle Ore-Mountains. It is worth taking a walk through the little village; the interesting church was built in 1799 as an octagonal central building with a double gallery round the interior. A visit to Seiffen is to be particularly recommended during Advent, for many of the Christmas traditions of the Ore-Mountains are still kept up here.

Chronological Table of the Town's History

Earliest settlement in the Elbe Valley between Pirna and Meissen during the Palaeolithic Age. During the Bronze Age spreading of the settlement areas on both sides of the Elbe. Around the time of Christ's birth the area was settled by the Hermanduras, a Germanic tribe.

929 After 400 years of Slavonic settlement, the German King Heinrich I invaded the Sorbic realm and conquered the Dalamintians, who lived between the Elbe and Saale Rivers; then he took the fortress of Jahna near Lommatzsch and founded Meissen Castle. This was the beginning of the Margravate of Meissen.

1089 The rule of the royal House of Wettin began when Heinrich I. of Eilenburg was enfeoffed as Margrave of Meissen.

circa 1200 A margravial castle is founded opposite the Sorbic fishing village of Drezdany, most of which is located on the left bank of the Elbe.

1206 Drezdany is mentioned as "Dresdene" in a document for the first time.

1216 First reference to Dresden as a town. To distinguish it from the village "Altendresden" (Old Dresden) on the right bank of the Elbe, the town developing on the left bank of the Elbe (first mentioned in a document in 1449) was called "Neuendresden" (New Dresden).

1234 A Chapel of the Cross is built for the relic of the Cross; in this connection first mention is made of the Nikolai Church, which since the 14th century has been called the Church of the Cross.

1275 The wooden Elbe bridge, at the same place as the present Augustus Bridge, is destroyed and rebuilt immediately afterwards with stone foundations.

1285 First mention of the castle.

1299 First mention of the town wall.

1309 Oldest known town seal.

1319 The Wettiners take possession of Dresden for good.

1349 Pogrom and expulsion of the Jews from the town.

after 1382 Margrave Wilhelm I enlarges and reinforces the castle considerably.

1403 Old Dresden is given its town charter.

1464 When the Dukes Ernst and Albrecht move to Dresden, the town becomes the residence of the Wettins.

1485 After the division of the country into an Albertine and an Ernestine part, Dresden becomes the residence of the Albertine line.

1491 A big fire destroys half of the town. Afterwards, new building regulations are enacted, which stipulate stone for corner houses and frontages up to the first storey, as well as tiled roofs.

1517 Martin Luther preaches in the Castle Chapel. Georg the Bearded opposes the Reformation.

1539 Introduction of the Reformation. The Church of the Cross and the Epiphany Church become Protestant parish churches.

1545 Dresden has 490 houses and 6500 inhabitants. A building regulation fixes the prices for wages and material and prohibits the keeping of livestock in the centre of the town.

1547 Duke Moritz becomes Elector – thus Saxony is now the most important Protestant state. Conversion of Dresden into a capital in renaissance style.

1548 Founding of the Court Orchestra, later to become the Dresden State Orchestra.

1553 The mint is moved to Dresden, its director is the mathematician Adam Ries.

1560 Founding of the Electoral Art Chamber in the Castle. Its contents form the basic stock of the special museums of the present State Art Collections.

1617 Heinrich Schütz is appointed court director of music in Dresden.

1676 The Large Garden is laid out by J. G. Starcke and court gardener M. Göttler.

1679 The oldest printed chronicle of Dresden (by Anton Weck) is published.

1685 Most of Old Dresden is destroyed by fire. Immediately afterwards, W. C. von Klengel draws up a development plan, later to become the basis of August the Strong's lay-out of the "new town near Dresden", the future Neustadt (New Town).

1694 Beginning of August the Strong's reign as Friedrich August I.

1697 August the Strong becomes a Cathloic in order to attain the Polish Crown. Saxony loses its leadership of the Protestant countries, but its union with Poland, at that time the second largest European country, enables it to rise to a great European power.

1699 Dresden has 21300 inhabitants.

1707 On the Jungfernbastei a laboratory is set up for the alchemist J. F. Böttger.

1708 Johann Friedrich Böttger invents European hard porcelain. Johann Melchior Dinglinger finishes work on the "Imperial Household of the Great Mogul".

1710 Founding of the Porcelain Manufactory in Meissen. Building work is started on the Zwinger, which is finished in 1732.

1719 Wedding celebrations on the occasion of the marriage between the electoral prince and the Habsburg imperial daughter Maria Josepha.

1720 Building starts on Pillnitz Castle to plans by Pöppelmann.

1723 Until 1736 Moritzburg Castle is completely renovated by Pöppelmann, Longuelune and de Bodt.

1726 Laying of the foundation stone of George Bähr's Church of our Lady.

1727 The Zwinger is used as a building for collections.

1729 Dresden has 46572 inhabitants.

1733 Death of August the Strong. He is succeeded by August II (August III of Poland).

1736 The equestrian statue of August the Strong (the "Golden Horseman") is put up on the Neustadt Market. The dome on the Church of Our Lady is completed.

1738 Building is begun on the Catholic Court Church to plans by G. Chiaveri. It is completed in 1755.

1754 August III buys the "Sistine Madonna".

1760 Bombardment of the town by the Prussians under Friedrich II. More than 500 buildings are destroyed (including the Church of the Cross, the Anna Church, the Brühlsche Belvedere and the Gewandhaus).
After losing the Seven Years' War, Saxony has to pay a large contribution to the Prussians.

1764 Founding of the Art Academy in the Fürstenberg Palace.

1785 Schiller lives in Dresden until 1787 as a guest of the Körner family and finishes "Don Carlos".

1806 Saxony becomes a member of Napoleon's Rhenish Confederation and is now a kingdom.

1809 The ramparts are razed on Napoleon's orders.

1813 Napoleon wins his last victory in the battle near Dresden.

1815 After the Treaty of Vienna Saxony is forced to cede three fifths of its territory to Prussia; this means a considerable loss of its political influence.

1817 Carl Maria von Weber is appointed Court Director of Music.

1828 The royal art collections are opened to the public.

1831 According to § 18 of the Saxon Constitution the collections are nationalized.

1834 Until 1849 Gottfried Semper works at the Art Academy as an architect and professor.

1839 The first German long-distance railway connection is opened up between Dresden and Leipzig.

1841 The opening of Gottfried Semper's first court theatre, which is destroyed by fire in 1869.

1843 Richard Wagner, who has lived in Dresden since 1842, becomes the

Court Director of Music. "Rienzi" (1842), "The Flying Dutchman" (1843) and "Tannhäuser" (1845) are performed for the first time in the Opera.

1847 Until 1854 the building of the gallery house at the end of the Zwinger, facing the Elbe. Designed by Semper.

1849 Dresden May Rebellion which is suppressed by Saxon and Prussian military. Because of their participation in the rebellion, Semper and Wagner have to flee from Dresden.

1871 Until 1878 the building of Gottfried Semper's second theatre under the supervision of his son Manfred, to take the place of the previous, destroyed building.

1889 Until 1891 renovation of the Castle in neo-renaissance style.

1905 Founding of the artists' society "Brücke" (bridge). First performance of "Salome" by Richard Strauss.

1908 Founding of the garden city Hellerau with the German Studios and the Festival Theatre. The garden city, planned by the architects Riemerschmidt and Tessenow, develops into a centre for artists and intellectuals (Jaques Dalcroze, Mary Wigman, Rainer Maria Rilke). First performance of "Elektra" by Richard Strauss.

1910 Through incorporation of numerous suburbs, now 548300 inhabitants of Dresden.

1911 First International Hygiene Exhibition. First performance of "Rosenkavalier" by Richard Strauss.

1918 Abolition of the monarchy. Dresden is now the capital of the Free State of Saxony.

1933 After the seizure of power by the National Socialists, Jews and Nazi opponents are ruthlessly persecuted and expelled. That was done to the head conductor of the State Orchestra, Fritz Busch, as well as the artist Otto Dix and the philologist Victor Klemperer. In September the notorious exhibition "Reflection on Decay in Art" was on show in the New Town Hall.

1933 At the beginning of the Nazi era Dresden had 642143 inhabitants.

1945 On February 13th and 14th Dresden was almost completely destroyed by English and American bombers. Until 1964 securing and rebuilding of the Zwinger. In early summer already, concerts and theatre performances take place again under the most primitive conditions.

1952 The abolition of the German states in the DDR means that a structure built up over centuries is broken down arbitrarily. The state Saxony falls into the districts of Dresden, Chemnitz (Karl-Marx-Stadt) and Leipzig. Dresden becomes one of a total of 14 district towns in the DDR.

1953 The rebuilding of the town centre begins with the laying of the foundation stone on the west side of the Altmarkt. At first it is influenced by the Stalinist architecture in the USSR; then, in the 1960's, that is followed by a partly simple, partly monumental modernity, which has no relation whatsoever to the gradual growth and architectural traditions of the town. The aim is the new layout of Dresden as a "socialist city".

1956 The Paintings Gallery is reopened in the Semper building of the Zwinger. The paintings, evacuated during the war, were originally transported to the USSR – probably as part of the reparations – but given back to Dresden later, as was the stock of the other art museums.

1959 At the instigation of the General Director of the State Art Collections, Max Seydewitz, part of those bricks of the Church of Our Lady are removed that were salvaged and prepared for the rebuilding. The originally undisputed restoration of this important building is now undesired. From now on the impressive ruins are looked on as a memorial to the destruction of Dresden.

1972 A further wave of nationalization affects numerous smaller and medium-sized private firms; this is, particularly for the building trade, disastrous. There is now nothing to stop the dilapidation of whole town districts.

1981 The Vatican decrees that Dresden become the diocesan town for the Dresden-Meissen diocese. The former Catholic Court Church is now a cathedral.

1982 After a discussion in the Church of the Cross several thousands of most-
13.2. ly young people with flowers and burning candles move in a procession to the ruins of the Church of Our Lady. The waiting police do not intervene. From now on the Church of Our Lady is a symbol of the peace and civil rights movement in the DDR. The Ministry of State Security increases its surveillance – especially of the numerous peace, environment, and civil rights groups within the Protestant Church.

1985 The lack of social reforms and the perceptibly increasing economic problems lead to more people wanting to leave the country. Compared with the DDR average, the number of applications in Dresden is high. On February 13th Carl Maria von Weber's opera "Freischütz" is performed at the reopening of the Opera, restored as a copy of the original – exactly 40 years after its destruction.

1989 About 3000 people temporarily occupy the Main Station; they want to
4.10. get on the trains bringing the refugees from the German Embassy in Prague to West Germany. As on the following days, there are violent clashes with the police, who clear the station.

5. 10. The police and the State Security try to disperse the increasing number of demonstations around the Main Station and the Prager Straße by force.

8.10. Through the mediation of Christoph Ziemer and Bishop Johannes Hempel of the Saxon Protestant Church, mayor Wolfgang Berghofer offers to talk to the demonstrators: this is an indirect legalization of the demonstrations by the state. During the next few weeks political happenings are determined by the "Gruppe der 20" (Group of 20) – its members were among the demonstators.

10.10.The Dresden press reports for the first time objectively on what is going on in the town. From now on demonstrations and political discussions take place permanently. There is a feeling of change.

9.11. During the next few days thousands of Dresden citizens wait in queues in front of the registration offices of the People's Police in order to get a visitor's visa for the Federal Republic of Germany.

19.12. Federal Chancellor Kohl meets Minister President Modrow in Dresden. There follows a rally in front of the ruins of the Church of Our Lady: tens of thousands of Dresdeners rejoice at the prospect of a united Germany.

1990 18.3. After a polemical election campaign, the first free parliamentary elections in the DDR are held. They are won by the "Allianz für Deutschland" (Alliance for Germany), an election alliance between the three conservative parties, CDU, DSU, and DA.

6.5. The CDU also wins the municipal elections. It appoints the new mayor, the computer scientist Dr. Herbert Wagner.

1.7. The temporary problems in connection with the monetary union are particularly hard for Dresden, as a town with a great industrial potential but hardly competitive. At the same time the community is faced with great financial problems. Even the closing of important museums and theatres is sometimes considered.

3.10. As from today, the constitution of the Federal Republic of Germany is also valid on the territory of the former DDR.

14.10. Reintroduction of the German states and state parliament elections on the territory of the former DDR. The State of Saxony exists for the first time again in 38 years. The CDU politician Prof. Kurt Biedenkopf is elected to be Minister President.

With good half a million inhabitants, Dresden is the 14th largest German city.

Fritz Beckert: The Towers of Dresden

Meissen, Albrechtsburg

Baroque Garden Großsedlitz

DRESDEN FROM A TO Z

ACCOMMODATION SERVICE
(Zimmervermittlung)

Dresden Information,
Prager Str., 8010 Dresden,
Tel. 4955025

ADVANCE BOOKING OFFICES
(Vorverkaufsstellen)

Zentrale Vorverkaufskasse
Schinkelwache am Theaterplatz
Tel. 4842333,

Kulturpalast Entrance Schloßstraße
Dresden Information
Prager Straße 10/11
8010 Dresden, Tel. 4955025

AGENCY FOR ARRANGING LIFTS
(Mitfahrzentrale)

Friedrich-Engels-Str. 10,
8060 Dresden
Tel. 51216

Concordienstr. 74, 8023 Dresden
Tel. 55493

ANTIQUES
(Antiquitäten)

Antiquitäten Rehefelder Str. 6,
8023 Dresden

We Buy and Sell,
Bautzner Str. 23,
8060 Dresden

Jentsch,
Elsa-Brandström-Str. 15,
8020 Dresden

Löwe, Kesselsdorferstr. 40,
8028 Dresden

Rausch, Otto-Buchwitz-Str. 91,
8060 Dresden

Antiques, Straße der Befreiung 17,
8060 Dresden

ARRIVAL

By car:
Dresden has a motorway connection and can be reached via the Hermsdorfer Kreuz or the Berliner Ring. From Czechoslovakia you take the major road 170 (border crossing-point Zinnwald) or 172 (border crossing-point Bad Schandau).

By train:
Several express and fast trains run daily from Berlin to Dresden. The rail links with towns in west Germany are being extended permanently. From Cologne, Essen, Hannover and Frankfurt you travel via Leipzig, from Stuttgart, Munich and Nuremberg via Chemnitz. A short while ago a direct rail link with Hamburg was opened up. Dresden has two main-line stations, the Main Station on the Altstadt side and the Neustadt Station.
Information: Deutsche Reichsbahn (German Railway), Tel. 470600/ 471502

By air:
The international airport Dresden-Klotzsche is located several kilometres to the north of the town centre. At present there exist direct flights to Amsterdam, Bourgas (BG), Cologne, Dortmund, Frankfurt/Main, Hamburg, Kiev, Moscow, Munich, Paderborn, Paris, Simferopol, Sochi, Stuttgart, Varna and Vilnius. German domestic flights are certain to be increased in the near future.
Airport Dresden-Klotzsche, Karl-Marx-Str., 8080 Dresden, Tel. 583141
Booking office:
Stadtbüro Deutsche Lufthansa
Hotel Bellevue, Köpckestr. 15,
8060 Dresden
Tel. 570852/56620

BREAKDOWN SERVICE
(Abschleppdienst)

Cossebauder Str., 8028 Dresden
Tel. 434050

Hans-Joachim Dornig,
Dohnaer Str. 72
8020 Dresden, Tel. 477062/479989

CABARET
(Kabarett)

Herkuleskeule,
Hans-Beimler-Platz 8010 Dresden,
Tel. 4955191

Dresdner Brettl,
Maternistr. 17, 8012 Dresden,
Tel. 4954123

CAMPING

Campsite Mockritz,
Boderitzer Str. 8, 8020 Dresden,
Tel. 478226,
with open-air pool

Campsite Moritzburg,
Am Mittelteichbad, 8105 Moritzburg,
Tel. 442

Campsite Reichenberg,
Am Sonnenland, 8101 Reichenberg am See

Campsite Scharfenberg,
Im Rehbocktal, 8251 Scharfenberg,
Tel. Meissen 2680

CAR HIRE
(Autovermietung)

Hertz Service, Hotel Bellevue,
Tel. 5662840

interRent-Europcar
Car repairs,
Liebstädter Str. 5, 8020 Dresden,
Tel. 2323399

Sächsische Taxi- und Fahrschul GmbH
Blüherstr. 9, 8010 Dresden,
Tel. 4951208

Autohaus
Bremer Str. 35, 8010 Dresden,
Tel. 437054

CHEMIST
(Apotheke)

Prager Str. 3, 8010 Dresden,
Tel. 4951320

DOCTOR ON CALL
(Ärztebereitschaft)

Automatic answerer 0160

DOCTOR ON EMERGENCY CALL
(Notarzt)

Tel. 52251

EMERGENCY NUMBERS
(Notrufe)

Police 110
Fire brigade 112
Ambulance 115

GALLERIES
(Galerien)

Galerie Comenius
Bautzner Str. 22, 8060 Dresden
Closed on Mondays

Galerie Gebrüder Lehmann
Institutsgasse 4, 8010 Dresden
Closed on Mondays and Tuesdays

Galerie Kunst der Zeit
Ernst-Thälmann-Str. 7, 8010 Dresden

Galerie Mitte
Fetscherplatz 7, 8019 Dresden
Closed on Mondays and Tuesdays

Galerie Nord
Leipziger Str. 54-56, 8023 Dresden

Galerie Ost/Leonhardimuseum
Grundstr. 26, 8054 Dresden
Closed on Mondays and Tuesdays

Galerie Rähnitzgasse
Rähnitzgasse 8, 8060 Dresden

Galerie West
Kesselsdorferstr. 70, 8028 Dresden

Kunstausstellung Kühl
Zittauer Str. 12, 8060 Dresden
Closed on Mondays

Neue Dresdner Galerie
Ernst-Thälmann-Str. 16,
8010 Dresden

HANDICAPPED PEOPLE'S HELP
(Behindertenhilfe)

Car service Tel. 5952222
Taxi Tel. 8133337

INFORMATION

Dresden Information
Prager Str. 10/11, 8010 Dresden
Tel. 4955025

LIBRARIES AND ARCHIVES
(Bibliotheken und Archive)

Sächsische Landesbibliothek,
Marienallee 12, 8060 Dresden
Tel 52677
Abt. Deutsche Fotothek,
Brühlsche Terrasse, 8010 Dresden,
Tel. 4954090

University Library of the TU,
Mommsenstr. 7 and 11,
8010 Dresden
Tel. 4633377

Zentrale Kunstbibliothek
der Staatlichen Kunstsammlungen
(Art Library)
Günzstr. 34, 8019 Dresden,
Tel 4593813

Staatsarchiv (State Archives)
Archivstr. 14, 8060 Dresden
Tel. 570680

Stadtarchiv
(Town Archives)
Marienallee 3, 8060 Dresden
Tel. 54750

LOST PROPERTY OFFICE
(Fundbüro)

Bautzner Str. 130, 8060 Dresden
Tel. 53484

PETROL STATIONS
(Tankstellen)

Autobahntankstelle
(Motorway petrol station)
Wilsdruff, 8224 Wilsdruff,
Tel. 0294-307 0 - 24

Wiener Str.
Corner Gerhart-Hauptmann-Str.,
8020 Dresden
Tel. 4706160 - 24

Bautzner Str. 93, 8060 Dresden
Tel. 517270 - 24

POST OFFICES (IN THE TOWN CENTRE)
(Postämter)

Postamt 1,
Am Queckbrunnen, 8010 Dresden,
Tel. 4953017
Mon.-Fri. 8 a.m. - 7 p.m.

Postamt 72,
Leningrader Str. 26 (Entrance Prager Str.), 8010 Dresden,
Tel. 4954165
Mon.-Fri. 8 a.m. - 6 p.m.,
Sat. 9 a.m. - 12 a.m.

Postamt 73, Main Station,
Tel 4848289
Mon.-Fri. 6 a.m. - 10 p.m., Sat.,
Sun. 7 a.m - 9 p.m

RACE COURSE
(Pferderennen)

Oskar Röder Str. 1,
8036 Dresden-Seidnitz,
Tel. 2371103

SECOND-HAND BOOK-SHOPS
(Antiquariate)

Dresdner Antiquariat,
Bautzner Str. 27, 8060 Dresden

Carl Mollers,
Brucknerstr. 28, 8053 Dresden

Dienemann
Antonstr. 35, 8060 Dresden

Ungelenk C. L. Nachfolger,
Plauenscher Ring 7, 8027 Dresden

Berti Hoffmann,
Oschatzer Str. 4, 8023 Dresden

SIGHTSEEING TOUR OF THE TOWN
(Stadtrundfahrt)

Short tour (90 min.)
daily 10.30 a.m.,12.00 a.m.,
1.30 p.m., 3.00 p.m., 4.30 p.m. from
Dr. -Külz-Ring

Long tour (3 hours)
incl. guided tour of Pillnitz Park.
Daily 10.00 a.m. from Dr.-Külz-Ring.

Short tour (90 min.)
daily 10.00 a.m., 11.30 a.m.,
1.00 p.m., 2.30 p.m., 4.00 p.m.
from Augustusbrücke (Augustus Bridge)

Tour by tram,
daily except Mon. 9.00 a.m.,
11.00 a.m., 1.30 p.m.
from the Postplatz

SWIMMING POOLS
(Bäder)

Indoor pools:
Sachsenbad,
Wurzener Str. 18, 8023 Dresden,
Tel. 52836

Schwimmhalle,
Steinstr., 8010 Dresden
Tel. 4593048

Schwimmhalle Prohlis,
Dohnaer Str. 135, 8036 Dresden,
Tel. 2743161

Schwimmhalle
Freiberger Str., 8010 Dresden,
Tel. 4951180

Open-air pools:
Arnhold-Bad,
Dr.-Richard-Sorge Str. 10,
8010 Dresden
(15. 5. - 15. 9.)

Bühlau open-air pool,
Bachmannstr. 6, 8052 Dresden
(15. 5. - 15. 9.)

TAXI

Tel. 4312
Tel. 4598112

YOUTH HOSTELS
(Jugendherbergen)

Hübnerstr. 11, 8027 Dresden,
Tel. 470667

Sierksstr. 33, 8054 Dresden,
Tel. 36672 (Oberloschwitz)

Weintraubenstr. 12, 8122 Radebeul

ZOO
Tiergartenstr. 1, 8020 Dresden
Tel. 475445,
daily 8 a.m. - 6 p.m.

DRESDEN

NEW

The new VIDEOGUIDE

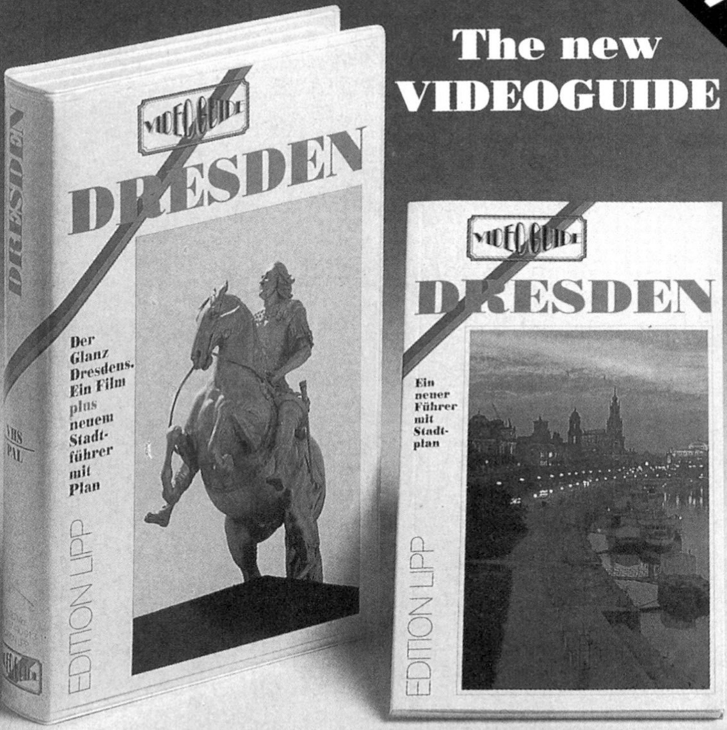

Video plus new town guide with street map.
The ideal way to plan your journey!

A coproduktion of EDITION LIPP with the David Menzhausen TV- and Video Production Munich.

Karl M. Lipp Verlag, Meglingerstr. 60, 8000 München 71
Telephone 0 89/78 58 08 - 0, Fax 0 89/78 58 08 33

Introduction price **DM 49.**

EDITION LIPP – THE MUSEUM VISITOR'S COMPANION

New productions are being prepared:
Red Indian Catalogue, Karl May Museum • Catalogue of Old Picture Postcards of Radebeul, Karl May Museum • Video Guide to the Porcelain Manufactury Meissen • Catalogue of the Stralsund Museum of Marine Biology • Seiffen Museum Catalogue, and many others.

KARL M. LIPP VERLAG, Meglingerstr. 60, 8000 Munich 71
Telephone: 0 89/78 58 08-0, Fax: 0 89/78 58 08 33